Martha's Story

Martha's Story

Martha Zeah Garkpi

Library of Congress Control Number: 2017916490
ISBN: Hardcover   978-1-5434-6109-1
                 Softcover   978-1-5434-6108-4
                 eBook   978-1-5434-6113-8

Scripture taken from the King James Version of the Bible.

Holy Bible, New International Version®, NIV® Copyright ©1973, 1978, 1984, 2011 by Biblica, Inc.® Used by permission. All rights reserved worldwide.

Any people depicted in stock imagery provided by Thinkstock are models, and such images are being used for illustrative purposes only.
Certain stock imagery © Thinkstock.

Print information available on the last page.

Rev. date: 11/10/2017

To order additional copies of this book, contact:

Xlibris
1-888-795-4274
www.Xlibris.com
Orders@Xlibris.com
767296

Pastor Kosiapoe Mercy Horace
15518 Silver Ridge Drive
Houston, TX 77090
Tel. 832-785-1287
mercyhorace1@gmail.com
www.mercyeducationalfoundation.com

Elder Martha Z. Garkpi, Author

ELDER MARTHA Z. Garkpi was born on December 15, 1949, in Zia, Lower Nimba County, Liberia. She was known to be a major pillar in every community in which she lived. She was very skilled and had many trades and titles to prove it. She was a wonderful mother, evangelist, and educator, striving to serve her people as God called her to do. She was an elder at Living Word Ministries International (Houston, Texas) and was also the matriarch of the church family. She taught at Calvary Baptist School, Living Word Academy in Monrovia, Liberia, and as well as the Alpha Child Development Center in Houston, TX. Ms. Martha's love for her people was apparent and a blessing in many lives. She spread her wings and flew home June 17, 2017, leaving behind this legacy and many people who loved her. As a result of her hard work, she was posthumously awarded a proclamation from Congresswoman Sheila Jackson (Texas) in July of 2017.

CO-AUTHOR'S INTRODUCTION

T O ALL OF the readers of this book, I pray that it is as powerful a blessing to you as it is to me. Seeing and living these events alongside my mother has worked wonders in my life and has showed me what God can do if you let him. My mother's courage, resilience, and strength are an example of His power. There is *nothing* too hard for God! He will see you through, no matter how tough the situation. My mother's life is a testimony to this. She truly lived her life for God, and He showed up and out in her life because of it. She had survived what many can't imagine, and her story is continuing to be told. Her ambitions came to fruition even after her passing. I say all of that to say this: when you submit yourself to him, he will make a way out of no way. Lay your burdens on him and leave them there!

Be blessed!

Pastor Kosiapoe Mercy Horace

DEDICATION

I DEDICATE THIS book to my family—daughters and son-in-laws, grandchildren, and all children placed in my care over the years.

I dedicate it to all of the women in the world. I dedicate it to all of my sisters, natural and spiritual.

Thanks to everyone who have helped in the writing process and in getting it in the hands of the readers.

My godparents, missionary Bill and Betty Thompson, whom I lived with within ELWA Liberia before I married—they are wonderful and caring people of God. God's blessing upon them.

Rebecca B. Mayu (my sister, my best friend)—she and I have come a long way in so many ways. She and I look like twin sisters. We understand each other very well. I appreciate God for our relationship. Thanks for everything.

Priscilla T. Debley was an encouragement to me starting this book project while in the United States. I had notes here and there for many years from many conversations. She brought me my first notebook and a pencil and said "Put them together." Thank you!

In loving memory of all my parents:

- My biological parents, Old Man Yarclay and my mother, Gbaiwon Z. Gbortoe
- My adoptive parents, Mealekpah Garkpi and Laiquee Seilone Garkpi
- My foster parents, Rev. John K. Demey and Mary Y. Demey[1]

Zobuia Wilson Yarclay, my brother, who was there for me as a young woman and when I got married, but passed away before this book could be published. May your soul rest in peace.

Ma Layziadiah Payla Niomie Joe (grandaunt) who was there with the Demeys in Tappita to help take care of me and my children. Thanks, Maiem, may your soul rest in peace.

Gray-Lay Goulou Wehyee[2]), my mother's cousin that I remember being very close to me and my children, I appreciate everything you did for me.

---

[1]   Mary Y. Demey, my foster mother who happens to have been my sister, is currently alive.

[2]   Gray-Lay Goulooe Wehyee, her cousin went home to be with the Lord before this book was published.

CONTENTS

THE OVERVIEW

My Mother's Wish—Leaving a Legacy

OUR MOTHER, A very devoted woman and a very caring jewel in the army of God, had indeed a very special story attached to her that needed to be told. The message she wanted to get across is very simple yet profound: women everywhere must be encouraged to take on Christ and stand in the midst of adversity.

For the past ten years, precisely when we opened the childcare center in Texas, my mother asked, "Kosiapoe, can you please type my book?" I answered; saying to her, "I will get to it when my workload is less," but the workload never became less.

I remember one day asking her, "Okay, where is the book?" She brought a stack of materials, and I asked my daughter Emmuel to type it. She was in the tenth grade then. She would type the book, and we would edit it at a later date. Again, with some daily circumstances, we lost track of it and never got back to it. She eventually stopped asking and began only relaying her story through conversations.

On June 3, 2017, we were having a family gathering, and we began asking her many questions. In the midst of our questioning, you could feel her becoming discouraged, knowing she would soon leave this earth. In that moment, sensing her thoughts, I reminded her that soon her story would be told. I promised her it was going to be completed, unaware of how soon she would be leaving me.

On Tuesday, June 6, 2017, she was not looking too good. In a moment of desperation, I called to her, "Sister" (a name I've been calling her since the day I could utter words). I asked her, "Sister, where is the book you were writing?" She said, "It is somewhere in here." I began to search everywhere and could not find it.

I called one of my sisters, Dayanah, and asked her if anyone had the manuscript.

She said, "No, I remembered seeing it, but I don't have it."

It was at this point that I got nervous. I said, "The book would not have just walked away. It needs to be found!"

I heard my mother saying, "Take your time to look. The book is in the room here."

I then sat down and prayed. "Lord," I said, "I am sorry for all the delay. Please help me find this document."

In no time, she turned and looked in a certain direction. I kept my eyes on her, and I looked at that particular place. It was right there in a backpack, all secured in a ziplock bag and numbered as book 1, 2, 3, and so forth, with dates and very detailed. At this point, there was excitement, and she began to smile. I reminded her of a sister who had moved to Louisiana and had written some books, and I knew if I reached her, she would be determined to help me type faster. The urge to write this book led me to contact this dear sister, Evangelist Margery, who could assist in the typing process. The message came as no surprise to her. When I called her, she said, "Wow! Elder Martha had asked me few years ago to type it for her, but I am on my way."

She arrived in Houston June 7 and began typing immediately. Day and night, she was working on the project. Elder Martha was very happy to see her. At some points, she was in the room with her as she typed.

This went on until Saturday, the tenth of June, when my mother Martha would not leave her bed. My husband, Bishop Bedell Horace, and I were unable to get her out the bed to the shower, which was routine for us.

She refused her breakfast that morning, and I began to be scared as to what was going on.

This particular day we had a street evangelism scheduled. I had to send for one of her spiritual sisters, Ms. Shirley Householder, to be some company to her in our absence. Looking at the situation that my mother was being faced with that morning was very troubling for me. She was asked to come at 12:30 p.m., but she came earlier at 9:00 a.m. This lady showed much kindness all during my mother's illness.

At this point, I'm getting ready for the evangelism. As I was getting prepared, my mother started looking noticeably different. Ms. Shirley would come and say, "Mrs. Horace, your mother doesn't look good." I continued to get ready, but already knew I would be taking her to be seen. I would tell her, "It won't be long. Let me get through with this." When more help arrived to assist in the evangelism transition, I called for an ambulance. On that day, June 10, my heart was so broken, torn apart in pieces. I was not willing to accept that she was on her way to glory. I was very nervous, hugging her and reminding her of her book that was being typed, and I told her that she had to be the one to endorse it. She would look at me and smile. I prayed so hard, but I didn't know what to say to God. There was so much that could be said.

"Sister, do not go anywhere. Why are you trying to leave me? We have so much to complete! Why?" I took her illness very personally, and I was very disappointed, knowing all the dreams she had to fulfill with me. She was a strong influence in the high school being built in Monrovia by my husband, Bishop Horace, and me. She had asked my husband and me to start her a house project in Tappita. She wanted to go in person and demolish her property in Monrovia and rebuild it herself. She wanted to go and fellowship once more in Liberia with her church family and other family members. She wanted to start a school in Tappita and also wanted to go and have a feast for all our ancestors who passed away during and after the Liberian civil war. Her trip was originally scheduled for February 2017.

"Oh, Sister, no! Please don't go!" I remember filming the last ambulance visit to our home. It was very sad. As I looked at her, I felt some hope. *Knowing her, she will be back in no time.* She dreamed of many things, but her illness was at a raging stage. The condition pretended to look good on blood work, but the cancer slowly caused her body to deteriorate. On June 13, her condition took a turn for the worse. I said to myself, "What will we do with the book whose material is being typed right now?"

As I looked at her each day, with little or much conversation between us, I said, "O God, my dream, her dream, our fulfilments!" Nothing could be done to further the progress of her dream. We could not even communicate with each other! I lived my mother's testimony. I, Kosiapoe Mercy Horace, endorse each testimony she has conveyed within her book. I live for her to be heard through me, so help me God. Being she is my angel now, I welcome her presence everywhere at any time that her story needs to be heard!

She had so many dreams . . . Dreams, dreams. . . Live on dreams . . .

My mother, Martha, was such a strong woman. She was very courageous and endured pain in such a dynamic way.

As a child, it was very tough for me to see all that she had gone through. As I looked at her then and perceive her now, my courage is even more zealous and stronger than before. My courage to take on this book project is beyond description because this is something she wanted so much. She valued her life in a very special way—even more than the way I saw it. It caused me pain to see this poor woman and how she had suffered all her life to get us where we are. That is not how she saw herself, though. She saw herself in a different light and always lived a life that showed it. I came to a strong belief that her faith was anchored on the solid rock and firmly holding to the infallible words of God. With blessed assurance, I reminded myself of the scriptures:

Present Suffering and Future Glory (Romans 8:18–31 NIV)

I consider that our [my] present sufferings are not worth comparing with the glory that will be revealed in us [me]. For the creation waits in eager expectation for the children of God to be revealed. For the creation was subjected to frustration, not by its own choice, but by the will of the one who subjected it, in hope that the creation itself will be liberated from its bondage to decay and brought into the freedom and glory of the children of God.

This is my joy: to know she was rich and wealthy in her lifetime. She was storing up for herself this legacy that will bless many. Picking up this material in my mourning state was a great challenge. I asked myself "Why me?" And then, I said, "Why not me?" This is a big responsibility, but there is a reason behind it. She knew that her battle was about over when she conveyed her book to me. She was in preparation of departure, and someone had to take the baton and run with it.

As this book spreads, please remember that it came through the process of pain, joy, travailing, and a lot of prayers. She was tested and challenged along life's journey, but she finished her course, and her job was well-done. Today the Savior has said to her, "Well done, my good and faithful servant. Enter your rest!"

Pastor Kosiapoe Mercy Horace (eldest daughter)

AUTHOR'S INTRODUCTION

THE STORY OF my life is dear to my heart. It tells of how God has always been there for me through all my life's challenges. The amazing grace of God is the story of a mother of four children who was abandoned by her husband, had survived fourteen years of a bloody civil war, and had lived to tell the story. It's indeed a blessing to share among women everywhere the story of my life and how I made it through the things thrown at me by the enemy of my soul. I learned to trust God early in my life. I could not have made it through the bombs set off in my life without him.

I have always had strong trust, faith, and belief in God! Who else could have carried me when I didn't feel like going on? Nobody but God! For sure God is there. He never leaves us or forsakes us. He is an amazing God! He is yet my strength today! My husband walked away from me and left me with four daughters. We were abandoned by the love of my life! I often wondered what I would do with myself and my daughters. What would I tell them? What would people think about me? I was so embarrassed! I am married, but now where is he? I decided to stay single for the testimony of my God and the love and respect I have for my children. Amid it all, I was victorious because God gave me grace to carry on. His grace was sufficient for me. His strength was made perfect in my weakness.

Here is where the journey began! I was launched out into the deep sea of loneliness and sorrow, but that's where I found a deep trust in the Lord Jesus Christ. Without him, I realized I could do nothing. Without him, I would have failed. With Christ now, I found that I could make it without submitting to the pain in my heart. I encourage every woman to turn to God for love and help. He will never leave you or forsake you.

CHAPTER ONE

The Story of My Life

M Y STORY IS not a unique one. Sorrowfully, many are faced each day with situations and circumstances that carry them off the course of life as God ordained for the woman. Martha, a single African mother faced with bringing up four daughters alone, which is sometimes unheard of. In my home country of Liberia, West Africa, family values were taken very seriously. Family was everything. You married young, submitted to your husband, and followed his lead.

I was born to the union of Gbaiwon Gbortoe and Kawien Yarclay on December 15, 1949, at the banks of a creek called Zuoeh-gbalea, in a small town called Zia in Tappita, Nimba County, in the eastern interior of my country. The people in that village went fishing once every year at Zuoegbalau Creek. My mother gave birth to me on that one special annual fishing trip. My life would be surrounded by miracles. I was born in a cold bush, on a green leaf, and was brought to town in a fishing net. I was born with two umbilical cords, which showed that I was a twin, but I was only one and very small! I was named Zeah, which means "Twin." They gave me a nickname Zeah Kue-duo-la ("Zeah on One Arm") because I was very small—people held me in one hand. Today people will call me a premature child. There were no hospitals to keep me under heat, but God kept me warm in his merciful arms. My biological parents came from two different towns from the one in which I was born. My father was from a neighboring town of Graie, and my mother from Zoiplue. After my birth in Zia, I was taken to my mother's hometown in Zoiplue. I was later taken back to Zia, where my miracle began, and then to the Mid Baptist Mission in Tappita City.

My Family Tree

Top Row (from left): Emmanuel Horace, Barkon Greaves, Marian Horace-Hill, Layziadiah "Niomie-Love" Horace, Michael Thomas, Emmuel Horace, Bishop Bedell Horace
Middle Row: Degusia P. Mulbah, Walter Mulbah, Judy B. Greaves, Martha Z. Garkpi, Dayanah B. Thomas, Pastor Kosaipoe M. Horace
Bottom Row: Bedell Debleye, Mary Greaves, Henry Greaves, Wasima M. Mulbah, Michael Thomas, Queen-McDyn Thomas

I would like to tell you all about my family names. My mother, Gbaiwon, had two children. I had a big brother—his name was Zobuia Wilson Yarclay—who was born in 1946 and died in a car accident April 9, 1972. My father's name was Kawien Yarclay, and my mother's name was Gbaiwon Zeagush Gbortoe. Her father's name was Mau-Gba Gbortoe. Her mother's name was Gaiyeai Wosiayata Gbortoe. My grandaunt's name was Mamie-Payla Layziadiah Niomie Joe. My aunt's name was Gouloun Quita Gbortoe. Grandpa Ma-Gba Gbortoe had a brother named Ziammay Gbortoe. My aunt Quetie Gonlone had two children: a son, Peayiamun Quetie, and a daughter, Yeemu- Wonla Quenlisi. I had one close cousin, Goulou Wehyee. My adoptive parents are the Garkpi family. My adoptive father's name was Mealekpah Garkpi. My adoptive mother's name was Laiquee Seilone. My adoptive sister, Mary Yeeyeah Demey, was married to Rev. John K. Demey, and they became my foster parents. Rev. Demey was born in 1924 and died in 2008. May his soul rest in peace.

I was around my mother's family more than my father's family, but I got to know most of them when I became older and married. I have lots of half sisters and brothers on my father's side.

My biological father was from Graie, and my biological mother was from Zoiplue, Voneah Town. I was born in Zia, and was taken to my mother's hometown, Zoiplue.

My three adoptive sisters' names are Mary Demey, Ruth Menlesh, and Lea Beapha.

God's Divine Plan

This is my testimony. I am a miracle child! It is almost impossible to fully narrate what God has done for me. This is the amazing story of my life. In 1952 an evangelist by the name of Mealekpeh Garkpi came to our village to preach the gospel. He had brought with him a box called a gramophone, which today is called a record player or sound system.

While the man of God preached, I fell asleep—not a regular sleep, but dead on my mother's lap at three years old. At the end of the sermon, when it was time to go home, my mother saw with surprise that I was not breathing. I was pronounced dead.

The town's people obliged the evangelist to pray me back to life if what he was saying about God was true. They threatened to do him bodily harm if he failed. They told him to open his box and pull my spirit out of it, according to their beliefs. The people took sticks at him to beat him to death. He asked if he could take the body in his room. They answered him, "Oh yes, it's okay." He took me in the room and laid me straight on a mat.

According to him, he then stretched over me and prayed, saying, "O God of Abraham, Isaac, and Jacob, you are the God of yesterday, today, and forever. Bring this girl to life so your name will be praised, for the people to know today that you are a miracle-working God." Within that time, at the end of the prayer, they said I sneezed and opened my eyes after many hours of intercession. I started crying and screamed very loudly, looking for my mother. The evangelist picked me up, raised me toward heaven, and thanked God for answering his prayer. He then went outside with me alive again and well, a miracle child.

When the people saw me in his arms, they started to run and said to my mom, "This girl is a living dead. Let this man take her away because she will not live for long." My family, fearing what people were saying, gave me over to the evangelist Mealekpeh Garkpi. They told him, "If Zeah became someone who was good, that will be your blessing. But if she be bad, that will be your bad luck." They said all was up to him and his God. I became the miracle child from God to Evangelist Garkpi and his wife, Laiquee Seilone, who could never have children. She was barren. From that moment on, I never entered my parents' house again.

My new mom took care of me. My biological mother often visited me as time went by. I was given to my adoptive parents, evangelists who came to the church to preach, after I died and was brought back to life because of the prayer of a threatened preacher. My family being afraid to take me home, they handed me to the man of God even though they prayed and tried to assure my mom that I would be okay. She was still in fear. Giving me away was just the beginning of God's plan for my life. I went to school earlier than most kids because my foster father, Rev. John K. Demey, was on the Baptist Mission board.

It was all in the plan of God for Laiquee Seilone Garkpi to care for me. As my new mom, she was very affectionate, and she really took care of me. Even in the absence of my biological mother, I still felt that mother's love.

Being given to my adoptive parents, the evangelists who came to the church to preach, was all in God's plan. Dying and coming back to life was in his plan as well. This family believed in God for a child of their own, and God answered their prayer through the transition in which I became their child.

Living with Pa Demey to attend school was in God's plan. He positioned Pastor Demey to be serving on the Mid Baptist Mission board while attending the Bible school to become a pastor. He served as a pastor for many years. He was born in 1924 and did a great work for the people of God.

After the death of my mother, a missionary by the name of Cain Greenfield and his wife came over to our house and asked for me to go and play with their kids and babysit their baby. My father agreed. For years, I was moved between one missionary to another, from the Mellish to the Greenfield to Ms. Darling Saulsor, to Ms. Joan Peckinpaugh, Ms. Steward, to the Holmes from Tappita Mid-Mission, to Soukoko from the Holmes and to the Thompsons at ELWA Monrovia. All of this was in God's plan.

Sing with me:

> God's plan for my life
> The devil can't erase it
> God's plan for my life
> It is something you can't change
> (Repeat 2x)
> Our life, the devil can't erase it
> No man can change it

God is still the same. He still performs the same miracles he performed in my life, in the life of any man today if you let him. All we must do is continue to trust in him that he can do it for us. He did all these things for me, Martha. He will do the same things for you. God always performs what he promises.

Sing with me again:

> My God loves me
> His love will never end
> He lives within my heart
> For my God loves me

> Everyone who asks receives and he who seek shall find and to him who knocks it will be opened. (Luke 11:10)

> I will praise you O Lord with my whole heart. (Psalm 9:1)

While living with the Demeys, I worked for some missionaries. The first missionaries, Godwin Mellish and his wife, were also teachers. I was in their care for about two years before they went to the United States, and I went back to my family outside the mission. I still went to school but not at the mission. My grandmother, Lueadie, moved to Tappita from the village to take care of me while I was going to school; because of her poor health, she had to be taken back to the village; and I was given back to my older sister Mary and her husband, Rev. John Demey. I now returned to the Mission for school again, where my brother in law, my foster father, went to Bible School. He is still preaching today.

A Mother's Love

When I was nine years old in Tappita in January of 1958, my biological mother came to see me. She stayed with us for about a week before leaving. I still remember her as tall, bright, and skinny, with beautiful long hair. My mother was a very pleasant woman. She cooked me some okra with a little half-dried meat, blackened rice, and corn for dinner the last night of that visit. I still remember the taste to this day. I had a nice time with my mother that night. She told me she had given her life to Christ after Pastor Demey preached to her. There was a joy in knowing Jesus. She began to advise me to get to know about Jesus and be a good girl that she could be proud of someday. I promised her I would. She instructed me to love the family and be very respectful—it would all be for my good, and when I became grown, it would help me. I also promised her. She advised me not to be sad. She was going to be coming more often after this trip, and I was very happy. Hearing all of that made me feel good.

The day she left, I felt something very strange about her, like she would not come to us again. She kept telling Pastor Demey, "Please take good care of Zeah. She is so dear to my heart. I will come and stay longer next time." She said "Don't lie to me, Pastor" about fifty times. Over and over she told him, "Please move Zeah from the government school back to the mission school so she can learn more about Jesus like what you said to me! Please! Please!"

My mother travelled through the neighboring town of Kpaituo. On her way back home, she stopped to visit with her elder sister, Quetie Gonlone, whose daughter had just given birth to a baby girl. She danced in celebration when she got there. They ate some food served to them, but immediately after eating, my mother began to feel severe pain all over her body. According to her sister, she started crying, calling my name, saying nobody should take me away from the godly family, because she knew that they will take good care of me. She soon passed away. The family respected her last wishes and left me with the Demey and the Garkpi families.

The day she died, I had a dream about my mother. In my sleep, I dreamed about the nice time we had together. She cooked, and we ate. I asked her to tell me more bedtime stories. I felt good in my sleep. The next day, I could not get up from bed. I was very sick and could not eat.

Thinking about my mom in my dream, I felt good and had hope that she would soon come to see me again.

The same day, my sister, Mary Demey, asked if I would watch her baby while she went out to get firewood to cook supper. So we went with her on the farm to get the wood. When we got to the farm, Victoria (the baby) was dancing and having fun. I laughed so much until my sister Mary told me to stop because she knew that I didn't feel well. Just then, I felt pain from my head again, and I began to cry. My sister Mary stopped what she was doing and took me to town. When we got to the house, we saw my uncle Meibeh coming and asking for Pastor Demey. When I heard his voice, I wanted to know why he had come. I saw people going into the house. As I went closer to hear what was going on, I heard people crying softly.

As I went in, all I could hear them saying was "Oh no, oh no, she was here just yesterday. That cannot be." At last Papa Garkpi, my adoptive father, came into the house, and he said, "Let's call Martha." All I could remember him say was "Don't cry. God gave you to us, and we are going to take good care of you. God knows why." I felt warm love from the arms of all the families. We were told that someone had poisoned my mother and that was the cause of death. She died very young. It was in God's plan to have me in safe, loving care before my mother died. She made sure I stayed with them, the godly family. All I could remember about her was that she was tall, bright, and skinny with pretty long hair. She was a fine-looking woman. I had a nice time with my mother during her visit, a special moment that every child looked forward to with their parents. She told me a bedtime story each night of the entire week of her stay.

My Path to Eternity: Salvation

It was through a missionary named Mr. Zebee that I came to know the Lord. He taught children's Sunday school one Sunday about "a good place and a bad place"—heaven and hell. The good place that had good people, bright light, happiness, and no death, he said, was heaven. If a person dies, you will see them again if you know the Lord Jesus.

The bad place that had a big lake of fire, with the bad people burning and crying all day and night, he called Hell.

I then asked him, "Will they die?"

He answered, "No! They will be in the fire for eternity, forever and ever in pain—burning in a fire hotter than any cooking fire anyone can imagine."

Because I knew how cooking fire burns and hurts if it touches you, I told him that I would like to go to the good place so I could see my mom. I also decided that I wanted to be happy and be a good person. It was at this point that I gave my life to the Lord. After four years, I was submerged in water and baptized.

He also taught us *Ephesians 6:1–2,* that children should listen and respect their parents—Mom and Dad—as well as older people. When a child does that, he will live long and enjoy life on the earth. If not, they will die young. This Bible verse stuck with me during the days of my youth. The preaching and teaching about heaven, the good place, and hell, the bad place with blazing fire, was imprinted in my memory and remains with me even until this day.

Walking in the Spirit has not been my bread and butter every day along the way. Thank God for parents who have been there for me, teaching me God's words.

According to *Proverbs 22:6,* parents are to train up a child in the way he may grow, and when he is old he will not turn away from it. Not only that—if we put the Word in their hearts and minds, the Word will never leave them. Parents, let us train our kids while they are young in the things of God. Giving them things—all the good things in life—is not all to parenting, but what they will be tomorrow in Christ is what will count in the end. They are our next leaders in times to come. God is good all the time. Let us sow that heavenly seed in our children. I can assure it will grow. Through my salvation, I was blessed to lead some of my family members to the Lord, and other members of my family whom I knew came to know the Lord as well. I am happy to know one day we will all meet at the feet of the Lord! Amen!

MARTHA ZEAH GARKPI

CHAPTER TWO

When You Think You Are Right

THIS IS HOW I met my dear husband Rufus. His mother died when he was much younger. The Holmeses went to Africa as missionaries. After some years, they moved into Tappita Mission to teach. It was there the Holmeses saw me working among some single missionary girls, like Darling Saulsor, and asked me to work with them. Sometime later, they introduced me to their son, Rufus. We became friends, and he asked me for a date. We dated for a few years, and he went to Booker Washington Institute (BWI), away from us to complete high school. He later moved to Monrovia.

During our days of dating, we never kissed or touched each other. There was nothing physical between Rufus and myself. Then he was out of sight. I knew out of sight was out of mind—because when he went away to a boarding school at BWI, I never heard from him.

In 1964, I met Joe Demey,[2] and he asked me for a date. We dated for two and a half years. We became physically active without being married, which was wrong in the sight of God. I became pregnant and delivered my first child on November 7, 1967, at 3:30 a.m.—a girl we named Kosiapoe Mercy (Blessing). I had just turned eighteen and was suddenly a young mother. I dropped out of school. I had to move into the village on Garkpi's' farm, where I spent my entire pregnancy. I only came to town Tappita for doctor's visits. During those periods, when you get pregnant, you were an outcast so as not to influence the other children. Joe was attending Konulah Mission on a scholarship. He too

---

2   Joe Demey was killed 1992, also in the war. May his soul rest in perfect peace.

was pulled out of school for the sin he had committed according to the belief and value they held. I was very sad for my actions and kept asking God for his forgiveness. I missed all my mission sisters. All the fun we had together now I could no longer join. I had to fetch water on my head more often and break firewood, and I pounded rice and cassava often to help with the household chores now. All my fun as a teenager was gone out of the window. I did all I could by the advice of some of the big girls to abort the pregnancy, but none worked because I was carrying purpose inside me. Such thoughts and behaviors were not in the will of God. I repented and asked forgiveness. I am so glad that God kept my little girl, Kosiapoe Mercy, safe inside me. She had brought so much joy to me. She is my sister, my friend, and whatever I want her to be. She thinks she is my protector—that makes me laugh sometimes.

Two years after having my first child, Kosiapoe, my parents sent me back to school. By that time I should have learned my lesson. Oh yes! I left her in the care of my grandauntie, Mamie-Payla Layziadiah Niomie Joe, who moved to Tappita to oversee of my well-being in the care of both the Demeys and the Garkpis. I was sent away to Suacoco to where we had some indigenous missionaries from the Mid Baptist ministry. A few mission girls at Suacoco were Darlene M., Sarah K., and my niece Hannah D., in the home of the pastor Cammue. We had some awesome experiences being away from our families and striving for a betterment of life. It was not too long after two years that God opened another door, and later I moved to ELWA in Monrovia, in the home of the Thompsons, some American missionaries. During this season of my life, I finally met Rufus in Monrovia, and we started to date once again. He introduced himself to my foster parents, Uncle Bill and Aunt Betty Thompson. We dated for two and a half years, after which we decided to get married September 30, 1971, at ELWA Monrovia.

Thank God for the Thompson family. They did for me all that parents could do for a child to get me on my feet. They married us up. When they returned to the United States, they remained in constant contact with me and have been a part of my family to this day. Aunt Betty and

Uncle Bill Thompson now live in Wheaton, Chicago. When I moved to the United States, they invited me to visit their home, and they also visited with me in Baton Rouge, Louisiana, where I stayed with my daughter Mercy and her husband, Pastor Bedell Horace. On their visit in Baton Rouge, Louisiana, we did a lot of wonderful things together. Their relationship means a lot to me.

The Joy of Marriage

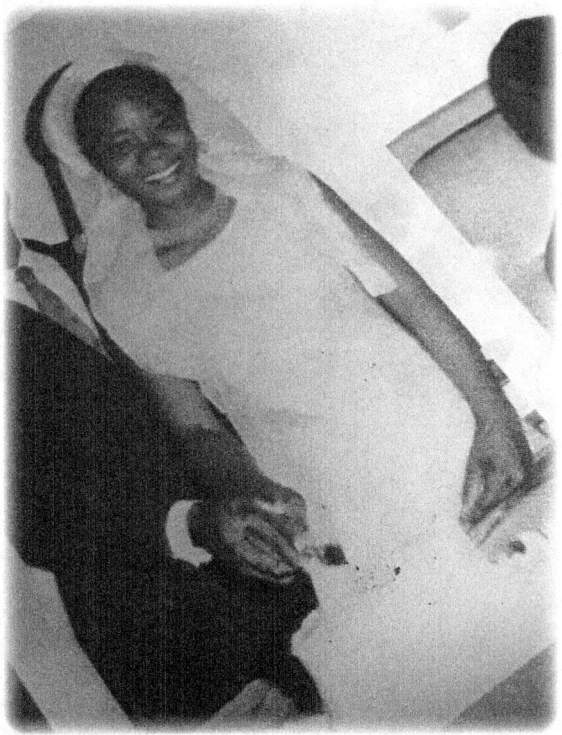

MARTHA ZEAH GARKPI

What a day that was! Marriage is a beautiful thing. I've always dreamed to have that fulfillment in my life as a young girl. My prayer was, "God, please bless my life as your Word has said." Please read with me:

- *Genesis 2:24.* "Therefore a man shall leave his father and his mother and hold fast to his wife, and they shall become one flesh."
- *Ecclesiastes 4:12.* "Though one may be overpowered, two can defend themselves. A cord of three strands is not quickly broken."
- *Mark 10:9.* "Therefore what God has joined together let no one separate."
- *Ephesians 5:25–33.* "Husbands, love your wives, as Christ loved the church and gave himself up for her, that he might sanctify her, having cleansed her by the washing of water with the word, so that he might present the church to himself in splendor, without spot or wrinkle or any such thing, that she might be holy and without blemish. In the same way husbands should love their wives as their own bodies. He who loves his wife loves himself. For no one ever hated his own flesh, but nourishes and cherishes it, just as Christ does the church."
- *Hebrews 13:4.* "Marriage should be honored by all, and the marriage bed kept pure, for God will judge the adulterer and all the sexually immoral."

My bridesmaid and maid of honor was Mrs. Martha N., and Mr. Melvin N. was a groomsman and the best man to my husband. Martha and Melvin are both husband and wife today, happily married with a lovely family, awesome careers, and a beautiful home—a dream that every couple hopes for, they had. I am proud of their commitment to each other. My godparents, the Thompsons, married us out. What a day it was, full of joy. Delicate tears came down my cheeks as my husband-to-be professed his love in front of everyone. I never thought anyone would or anyone could ever be in love as deeply as both of us. Weddings are meant to be wonderful, memorable, and exciting days that we were prepared for. I was relaxed to enjoy the day that we both had worked so hard for and had long been waiting for—to make things right with God and prove to my family they are wrong and I am right. We had special people at our wedding that came to share the special day with us. They were there to show their love and support to us, and to help make our day special and memorable. I remember till this day taking every second of those feelings in and embracing it, hoping that we will spend the rest of lives together. No one would ever hope for such good memories to turn into bad experiences. Our vows made everyone's emotions run wild. There were happy tears from us. We were happy to have our family and friends at our wedding.

Nightmare after Marriage

After my marriage, my nightmare in life really began. I would like to say to any young woman, when your parents say no to something, *listen* to them, especially when they have godly wisdom. Please read *Ephesians 6:1–2*. "Children, obey your parents in the Lord, for this is right. 'Honor your father and mother,' which is the first commandment with promise." Whenever children listen to their parents, things go well with them. In Africa, the old people have a saying, "The child who can't hear can't feel." This is a true saying. I live to see it daily.

Just one year after the birth of our child Judy on September 1, 1972, a year exactly after our wedding that we were so happy about, my nightmare began.

As I could remember, my parents did not even approve the marriage, but I told them that I loved him anyway and he loved me too. It was now already late at this point. I had made the worst decision of my life, but I never knew. My mistake and disobedience to my parents resulted in my lonely life today. Besides, I did not listen to my heart either.

Sometimes the signs of discord are right in front of you, but you choose to look beyond them. A friend once told me of a story that happened in her family. A month before her cousin's wedding, her cousin went to visit her fiancé, because he hadn't to visit her, nor had he answered any of her notes she sent him. She was suspicious that he was having an affair, but he denied all accusations. He even went as far as pulling out one of the notes that she had supposedly written to him, stating that he had already written a reply to it. When she opened the letter to read it, she found that it was addressed to another woman by the name of Netty. It was something to see. I asked what she did. According to the friend, the cousin forgave the fiancé, and they got married. I went "Wow!" thinking that he was sorry for his behavior and he was not going on the path again. No! That was all the beginning of her sorrow that she did not forsee from far off. When she told me of her experience, it took my mind back to similar experience I had. I said, "Oh goodness, this should have taught me a great lesson also," but I was not listening to my heart, and neither to the voice of the Holy Spirit. I went ahead and married anyway, against the advice and will of my parents. Others as well as family members kept saying "A child that can't hear can feel.

I was teaching at Calvary Baptist Elementary School with lots of wonderful people, and I was excited to show my love after work to one of my coworkers, who happened to be like a family member. You invite people into your home and open yourself to them with all good intentions, not knowing what is coming after. Some could be detrimental to your children, your job, your friends, your marriage, your godly lifestyle, and so forth. The mistakes I have made in lines of some relationships, I don't want you to make. I am kindly asking you to deeply consider asking the Holy Spirit for deep directions of who you bring into your inner circle. This includes the would-be parents of your children.

Pregnancy is one of the most delicate times for a woman, so I encourage the bonding and support between the parents of the child. Being in a good and faithful relationship with each other does matter greatly because there will be an influence on the child, whether both parents are active in their lives or not. Abandonment runs rampant in our communities as if it is the new cultural norm. We have to break this generational curse, starting with loving God, ourselves, and the one we are with first and foremost. Where there is no love, there will be turmoil. Instead of dealing with the loneliness, I had to focus on my children. I worked so hard to meet the children's needs. I had to make and sell pastries in the neighborhood and also in the front of Calvary Baptist School to provide for myself and the children. I worked and sent all four of our kids as well as other family children to school, because I worked at the same school that my children attended. Their fees were taken out of my salary each pay period, little by little, until the fees were completely paid out. Besides these fees, I paid rent, light bills, hospital bills, and took care of the entire family and my other relatives. It was a lot for a single mother, but God—God was my helper, and he stayed close to us in our challenging days, day after day. He is still my helper to this day.

God did an amazing thing. While I was still pregnant, there came a time that our lights were disconnected for about six months. My kids and I lived in the dark. I could not restore the lights because we did not have enough money to spare. I had to let it go like that, and the house would be very hot all the time. I will tell you about God's miracle. The moment that the lights went off, God put one air conditioner in the entire house. It was amazing. One hot afternoon, my husband passed by. When he entered the house, he knew that our lights had been off for a long time, but the house was very cool. He asked me, "Do you have lights now?" I replied, "No, why?" He answered, "Because your house is very cool." I told him, "God cooled it for me," and he walked out, never to return until I was in my ninth month of pregnancy.

He came with his uncle, Mr. D., to take me out that night. I said no, but because of his uncle, I decided to follow them. I called all our kids and told them, "Your father is taking me out with his uncle. If anything happens to me, he's the one you look for." We all laughed about it, and we went out that night and ate. When I came back that night from the dinner, I became very sick and was taken to ELWA hospital, where I stayed for about a week.

The Forces of Darkness

One night at the hospital, I had a dream. In my dream, I was taken to my home church in Tappita. People came from all over like for a funeral. After the church service, people started coming out of the church two by two. While they were coming out, I saw some people I had grown up with: Alice F., Louise F., and Judy W. In this dream, I was sitting at the side of the crossroads facing the original Tappita market. As people passed by, they began to laugh at me.

I asked one of my friends, Judy D., "Why are you all laughing at me?"

She said, "I don't know, but Darcy said we should laugh." Judy D. said, "Please, I am very sorry, Martha."

The next thing I knew, someone unexpected showed up in my dream. Right away I saw a baby girl beside me, and the baby said to me, "I came for you, and I too will fight you." The baby started squeezing my feet.

In prayer and in anger, I said, "No, Lord! I must live."

Then I was reminded of this battle that the prophet Nehemiah had to fight against the enemy of progress Sanballat, Tobiah, the Arabs, the Ammonites, and the people of Ashdod. Remember this is a spiritual battle, a fight against the purpose of a child born with two umbilical cords, carried to town in a fishing net, died to be raised by a barren evangelist, and going on to be left in the hands of total strangers all her life. Now the devil is mad, using good people to become the devil's assigned agents to take her out before the fullness of time. Not until God says so.

> But when Sanballat, Tobiah, the Arabs, the Ammonites and the people of Ashdod heard that the repairs to Jerusalem's walls had gone ahead and that the gaps were being closed, they were very angry. They all plotted

together to come and fight against Jerusalem and stir up trouble against it. But we prayed to our God and posted a guard day and night to meet this threat. Our battle against those that have chosen themselves to be our enemy is not over till God says so. They are prepared to fight till the end.

Therefore, I stationed some of the people behind the lowest points of the wall at the exposed places, posting them by families, with their swords, spears and bows. After I looked things over, I stood up and said to the nobles, the officials and the rest of the people "Don't be afraid of them. Remember the Lord, who is great and awesome, and fight for your families, your sons and your daughters, your wives and your homes."

When our enemies heard that we were aware of their plot and that God had frustrated it, we all returned to the wall, each to our own work.

From that day on, half of my men did the work, while the other half were equipped with spears, shields, bows and armor. The officers posted themselves behind all the people of Judah who were building the wall. Those who carried materials did their work with one hand and held a weapon in the other, and each of the builders wore his sword at his side as he worked. But the man who sounded the trumpet stayed with me.

Then I said to the nobles, the officials and the rest of the people, "The work is extensive and spread out, and we are widely separated from each other along the wall. Wherever you hear the sound of the trumpet, join us there. Our God will fight for us!"

MARTHA ZEAH GARKPI

So we continued the work with half the men holding spears, from the first light of dawn till the stars came out. At that time I also said to the people, "Have every man and his helper stay inside Jerusalem at night, so they can serve us as guards by night and as workers by day." Neither I nor my brothers nor my men nor the guards with me took off our clothes; each had his weapon, even when he went for water. (Nehemiah 4:17–18)

God has given us greater power to know that the battle is not ours, but his. With all my strength and courage, I started beating on the head of the baby in my dream until the baby died. I knew that this was a spiritual battle. While all this was going on, I had passed out in the hands of the nurses. They were fighting to bring me back to life, but God brought me through.

When I came through, about a week later, I gave birth to a dead baby girl. In real life, the baby's head was busted. It was like she had no head. She looked just like the child I saw in the dream. I knew that this was a spiritual battle, and that God had fought the forces of darkness on my behalf. According to the delivery nurse and my sister Rebecca M., who also worked in labor and delivery, the child's umbilical cord was already detached from the baby, and the front of the baby's abdomen was deformed at birth.

About three weeks later, my children and I were having our evening prayer. Suddenly, I felt a prick on the thumb of my right hand. It started to itch, and it began to swell and became very painful. I was in pain all night and throughout the next day. My daughter took me to JFK Hospital, and my finger was operated on. The next day, the finger had swelled more than it had the day before. I said, "Lord, here we go again." I had not fully gained balance from the other battle, yet I was now engaged in another one. But as we know, the devil is like a roaring lion (even though he is not a real lion)—he continues to seek whom he may devour. What he did not know was that I was on a mission best known to my eternal father.

In the midst of my hand pain, I began to experience some abdominal pain. I was taken to ELWA Hospital, and my doctor, Dr. Bob S., examined me and said I needed to have an urgent DNC because of some infection that had gone through my body since the stillbirth of the child I had. He said that I needed my husband to give his approval to do the work. I was sent home to come the next day. When I got home, I sent for one of my husband's sisters, and I asked her to look for her brother. I had a very important message for him. She went to his girlfriend Darcy's house, found him, and brought him to my house. There was not a positive response, nor any help. No one could assist me financially with the procedure. At this moment, I knew I was in this alone. Even though I was there for everyone else, no one was willing to be there for me. Even immediate family members, knowing my situation, treated me as if I were some pile of garbage. But in the midst of this storm, I managed to thrive. I kept the faith, and God moved on my behalf. I may not have gotten what I needed, but I had to trust the Lord. Just as quick as my husband came, he left.

My children kept me up, giving me water all night because my mouth was dry and I was passing out on them frequently. The next day there was no one to take me to the hospital, and it was raining. I looked too sick, so my eldest daughter, Kosiapoe, told me, "Sister, I will go and find a taxi to take you to the hospital." She did. At the hospital, Dr. Bob S. asked for my husband again as he had before. Then, because of my condition, I had to give him the permission to do whatsoever was necessary because I had no one else to sign for me. He proceeded to give me the DNC, and everything went well.

While I was at the hospital, Kosiapoe walked to school daily along with her little sisters. She was only thirteen years old at the time. My other daughters—Bley (9), Deyanah (7), and Degusia (6)—were very young, but they all took care of me.

Not Time Yet

When it's not your time to die or leave this world, no one or nothing can be the cause of it because God always has a way out. When I got to the hospital, Dr. Bob Schindler asked if I had eaten or drank anything since 12:00 a.m. I replied "Yes." He asked Dr. Trobe to keep his eyes on me for a few hours, but because of my condition, he went ahead and did the procedure anyway. By the grace of God, everything went just right. A wonderful doctor he was. After the operation, I began to have another infection on my finger. I did everything, but my finger still would not get better. The doctor cut it open again and again to let out some of the bacteria, but nothing helped the situation. At last I turned to God instead of the doctors, and he healed me. As God says in His word, "Call on me and I will show you great and mighty things that you know not of."

God worked through a woman, a nurse's aide named Ms. Youngua, who told me a story about the same thing happening to her. It was the work of an evil one. She boiled water and added salt and kept my hand in it until the water got cool. She did that three times a day for three days. That was it, my hand got better! God worked in the intervention of the nurse's aide, who in my eyes had to be an angel. Please, as you are listening to me, I am not bringing you to a place to give any glory to darkness. But be reminded that there is a real devil who works through willing vessels as agents to bring an end to a plan that God has for you. Are you familiar with the story of Job? I believe most people have heard about the brother Job—how he was tested and proven to be a great servant of God. The devil is real, and an adversary that we can't ignore.

Crippled, but Not Forsaken

One beautiful morning in 1984, I was heading to take two of my girls to school, Calvary Baptist Church School, which was also where I worked. I needed to get them there on time. When we got on the road to cross the street, I saw a taxi coming toward us.

We stopped, and then the taxi driver stopped also. He signaled us to cross because it was safe to cross the street. When we got to the center of the road, on the yellow line, the same vehicle began to advance toward us. The car picked me up and threw me down. While I was on the ground, I saw the car coming right over me and one of my daughters. There was a divine presence that came upon me. I suddenly pushed the vehicle right from over us. At that time of the morning, no one was on the road, and there were not many cars either. The taxicab driver was about to run away from the scene, just at the same time a strange man came from nowhere. Seeing the situation, he told the driver to stop and help assist me into the vehicle, and he did. This man took my two kids alone with him, and I rode in the same vehicle that hit me. He laid my head on his lap while I was being rushed to the hospital. He comforted me, telling me that it was going to be all right and to hold on in getting to the hospital. As we approached Twentieth Street, before turning into the John F. Kennedy Hospital, the stranger who helped me then told the driver to stop in view of a police officer. He got out of the vehicle and reported what he saw. He then walked alongside the police officer to the vehicle, and the officer told him to get in the vehicle as we got ready to enter the hospital. In that very moment, this stranger had disappeared. He could not be found anywhere. The officer asked me if I knew him. I replied, "No." Psalm 91:11–12 says, "For He God will give his angels charge concerning you, to guard you in all your ways. They will bear you up in their hands, that you do not strike your foot against a stone." God immediately sent this angelic being to come and save us during this accident.

Daniel 6:12 says, "My God sent his angel and shut the lions' mouths and they have not harmed me, inasmuch as I was found innocent before him; and also toward you, O king, I have committed no crime." God stopped another premature death in my life.

The policeman then took us into the hospital with the report he was given by the unknown helper who had miraculously come and then gone. I was treated, and the cab driver promised to look after me while

I was being treated. He kept his word. After treatment, I was taken home. We never saw the driver again. He could not be found anywhere in Monrovia.

One year later, I was still suffering from injuries from the accident. I was paralyzed.

This accident left me crippled for almost two years! I was stuck lying down in bed and needed the help of loved ones. I moved from one hospital to another and was not getting any better. There was no way I could work, go to church, or care for my children as I wanted, and I felt like I had no future. All of this was too much on my mind. Through it all, I continued to put my trust in the Lord to do it for me.

The Lord never ceased to amaze me in all the wonderful things he has done for me. One beautiful morning, my brother-in-law, Victor Martor, went out to look for a vehicle to come visit me at the hospital. The first car he saw was the same taxicab that had hit me a year ago. He asked the driver to bring him to the hospital.

When they arrived at the hospital, he called the police on the taxi driver. At this point, the driver was trying to deny the allegations to the police officer. He claimed that he was not who Victor was talking about, and he did not know what his passenger was accusing him of. The police officer said, "Let's go see this woman in question." When I saw the driver I was shocked! During this time, I was in bad condition, even worse than the year of the accident. The driver was taken to the justice to pay for pain and suffering. He was informed that he would go to jail if he did not comply with the demand. The driver agreed to do so. May God richly bless my spiritual brother, Victor Martor, who stood with me and the girls until he got married. May God bless their union with all that they desire. After two years, God miraculously set me back on my feet to care for my children as I should. When in battle, or not in battle, keep this verse in mind: "But we have this treasure in earthen vessels that the excellence of the power may be of God, and not of us. *We are* troubled on every side, yet not distressed; *we are* perplexed, but not in despair; Persecuted, but not forsaken; cast down, but not destroyed" (2 Corinthians 4:7).

Satan's Temporary Pass

Job 1:6–12 says,

> Now there was a day when the sons of God came to present themselves before the Lord, and Satan also came among them. The Lord said to Satan, "From where have you come?" Satan answered the Lord and said, "From going to and fro on the earth, and from walking up and down on it."

Do you understand this dialogue above? God knows our position and what we are capable of in terms of our faithfulness and stability to his service.

> And the Lord said to Satan, "Have you considered my servant Job, that there is none like him on the earth, a blameless and upright man, who fears God and turns away from evil?" Then Satan answered the Lord and said, "Does Job fear God for no reason?"

I came to realize that all that I was battling was for a reason. I knew who was behind those forces—not a person. They were just being used as agents. Ephesians 6:12 says, "For we wrestle not against flesh and blood, but against principalities, against powers, against the rulers of the darkness of this world, against spiritual wickedness in high *places*." This battle is against Satan.

> "Have you not put a hedge around him and his house and all that he has, on every side? You have blessed the work of his hands, and his possessions have increased in

the land. But stretch out your hand and touch all that he has, and he will curse you to your face." And the Lord said to Satan, "Behold, all that he has is in your hand. Only against him do not stretch out your hand." So Satan went out from the presence of the Lord.

Job 2:7–9 (ESV) continues with the following:

> So Satan went out from the presence of the Lord and struck Job with loathsome sores from the sole of his foot to the crown of his head. And he took a piece of broken pottery with which to scrape himself while he sat in the ashes.

Satan is very mindful of his techniques, but it is clear in our lives that the enemy has no power over us. What he thinks he has is only allowed by God, and it is only a temporary access for the purpose of testing our love for God. When we remain faithful, we give God the authority to remind the devil that he has no power and he is a liar.

> Then his wife said to him, "Do you still hold fast your integrity? Curse God and die." But he said to her, "You speak as one of the foolish women would speak. Shall we receive good from God, and shall we not receive evil?"

In all this, Job did not sin with his lips. When my body was going through all those trials, some people had so much to say. All I did was sing hallelujah anyhow. My fear was not in what man could do to me, but how faithful I could remain. Like Job 13:16 KJV says, "Though he slay me, yet will I trust in him: but I will maintain mine own ways before him." Let's be encouraged to remain faithful to God. John 8:48 KJV says, "Ye are of *your* father, the devil, and the lusts of your father ye will do. He was a murderer from the beginning, and abode not in the truth, because there is no truth in him. When Satan speaks it is all a lies, he speaks of his own: for he is a liar, and the father of it."

The devil is real, but we serve a greater God. God always protects us and shows us when the devil is trying to destroy us. You will know when some things just don't line up. Stay prayed up, and you will be just fine.

I was in the hospital for two weeks, and my husband Rufus did not come to see me until I went home. Amid all the challenges my husband was putting me through, his girlfriend Darcy was also pregnant. He had promised her a house if she had a boy child. She did give birth to a boy, and he built her a house immediately. She gave birth to another boy, and he built her a second house. Children are blessings no matter the gender, so I felt that this was unfair to the children. This made me realized that not everyone you want will be compatible with you, and that is okay. God gave us free will for a reason, and we have to learn to accept the choices that others are free to make. We also have to learn to be amicable in our dealings with each other, even if they aren't pleasing, and most especially if the youth is involved. We have to remember that at the end of it all, we are on the same team.

All this was being done while I was still his wife and lived in a rented house with his children. His actions toward me were shameful. From what I know, a woman does not determine the sex of the child, but he claimed I only produced girls and his name will die.

> According to Amy Johnson, Stanford University, X (or Y) marks the gender.

> Both men and women have sex chromosomes. Men usually have one X and one Y chromosome, while women have two X's.

> When an egg or sperm is made, it only gets one of the sex chromosomes from the parent. This means that

women can only make eggs with an X chromosome. But men can make either X or Y sperm.

During fertilization, the sperm cells race toward the mother-to-be's egg cell. If a sperm with a Y beats all others, then the fetus will be XY. The pregnancy will result in a boy.

However, if a sperm with an X wins the race to the egg, then the fetus will be XX. The parents will have a baby girl."

This is reason I have had all these girls, and I say this for the understanding of some parents who have been blamed in some ignorant cultures. Take courage and enjoy your children, ladies. We have no control of the sex of our children.

I had a run-in with a woman whom I happened to have known very well. I saw her and her grandmother in the street one day. Since I knew the family, I decided to speak to her grandmother. While talking with this older lady, the granddaughter came up from behind me and slapped me in my face two times. I tried to get away from her, but she threw a large block at me and cut me in my back. I was taken to ELWA Hospital for the wound, and I got very sick. I was tended to by a very kind nurse at this hospital. They found out that the cut had given me tetanus, which almost killed me. When she assaulted me, she used the opportunity to tell me everything she had been doing to me, and warned me that it was not over yet. She openly confessed over and over again, like she was very proud of what she was doing.

All these battles wore me out. They were not intended for me—why I saw myself in them, I have yet to know. I washed my hands of everything, as there was nothing that I could do for myself at this point. I had realized that not every battle you found yourself wounded in is yours. Sometimes you need the Lord's heavy artillery on your side. I had seen that I needed the Lord's salvation badly. I came to the point that I asked God daily.

The assault and threats she made were reported to the authorities. This happened because it was made in the presence of other witnesses, and she was arrested. She had done too many things to me during her relationship with my husband. There are not enough words to express all that was done. When you allow the devil to take you for a ride, he will put on a show. I lost my sanity behind all of this, because the enemy was relentless. The Bible says that the devil comes to kill, steal, and destroy, and it seemed that it wouldn't stop until the devil was victorious.

When my attacker got out of jail, my husband made sure to set me up to go where his girlfriend came from. He came and told me, "Martha, I will love to come back home tomorrow. Please come and get my things from Lucy's house. I am sorry. I am ready to come home."

I was very excited. Early that morning, I gathered some of the ladies in the community and asked them to accompany me to get to my husband house and bring his things. This was in 1981. When we arrived on the premises, we found that I had been set up. Everything that was told to me concerning the move was make-believe. I learned a major lesson that day, and I knew I was wrong to make the move to begin with.

However, we got there, and I proceeded to her and said, "I came to get my husband's belongings. He said that he no longer wanted to be with you. He was sorry for all he had done to me."

She replied, "For real Wait for me." She too gathered her forces, and this turned out into a fight between the ladies who went with me and the ladies she gathered. The scene was very chaotic, and in the midst of it all, the authorities were called. When confronted about my presence, there was a barrage of denials. Apparently, I wasn't asked to come, nor was I acknowledged. As a result, we were detained because of a violation of property laws. What a day—it was just like yesterday. I began to wonder why I believed this man. What have I gotten myself into, leaving my children at home? I said a thousand and one things to myself. When we were in jail, Kosiapoe, my daughter, had come from her vacation job. She was informed that something happened with some of the ladies in the yard. When she arrived, she was very saddened to see where we were. She said "Sister, you will get out" through tears. She gave all of us the assurance that we were coming out. All this happened over the summertime, when all the children were out of school. All this was the work of the enemy. It was still not my time. God kept his protection around and above me.

God has been good to me and my children. All I can say at this point is, whatever goes around comes around and nothing lasts forever. I was excited to see how God was going to turn it around for my good. I had all the assurance that whatever is for you in life will always seek your face. I was prepared to wait on the Lord's timing for everything. We must realize our mistakes are not stains that cannot be erased by God. Neither are our mistakes. He's not up in the heavens, shaking his head, saying, "I dreamed they would do that. They've ruined my plan for them." No, God knew every mistake we would ever make. He knew every wrong turn, and he's already prepared a new route. He already has your detour figured out. Even in the mistakes I made in marriage, when my parents disapproved, there was another route to walk on, which was on *Faith Street*. I knew that there was something higher than me that I was reaching for. Faith Street was the best detour ever, even though it was lonely. It was what was best for me. It kept me faithful to God and close to my children.

The scripture says that God knows the end from the beginning. If you've made some mistakes, the good news is that he has already planned a way to get you back on track. His word says "Come now, let's settle this," says the LORD. "Though your sins are like scarlet, I will make them as white as snow. Though they are red like crimson, I will make them as white as wool." Just come to him with an open and humble heart. Let him wash you clean and make you new. Your mistakes aren't bigger than God. He loves you and has a good plan in store for you. So if you have wronged someone, make it right with God and with them.

Sing along with me:

> Though your sins be scarlet
> Though your sins be as scarlet,
> They shall be as white as snow (Repeat)
> Though they be red as crimson,
> They shall be as wool;
> Though your sins be as scarlet, (Repeat)
> They shall be as white as snow. (Repeat)

Many days and nights, when I was lonely and hurt, these scriptures helped me find comfort in God. God has always been with me.

> Wait on the Lord; be of a good courage and he shall strengthen thine heart. (Psalm 27:14.)

Never look at your physical battle to turn to any evil force to get an even result. You will be playing on their playing field, and for sure you will lose. I have promised my God and myself that no matter how long it takes, I will wait. My grandson Emmanuel loves to sing this song and I am is always blessed by it.

> I'm waiting, I'm waiting on you, Lord
> And I am hopeful, I'm waiting on you, Lord
> Though it is painful, but patiently I will wait
> And I will move ahead, bold and confident
> I'm waiting, I'm waiting on you, Lord
> And I am peaceful, I'm waiting on you, Lord
> Though it's not easy no, but faithfully, I will wait
> Yes, I will wait

The eyes of all wait upon thee; and thou givest them their meat in due season. Thou openest their hand and satisfies the desire of every living thing. (Psalm 145:15–16)

He heals the brokenhearted and binds up their wounds. (Psalm 147:3)

The eternal God is your refuge, and underneath are the everlasting arms. He will drive out your enemies before you, saying, "Destroy them!" (Deuteronomy 33:27)

These scriptures always helped me get through my internal struggles. It is God that giveth life and taketh away life. Nobody can take your life. It belongs to God.

CHAPTER THREE

When God Says Yes

WHEN RUFUS AND I were married, we lived in rented houses from behind City Hall, ICA Camp, Twenty-First Street, Seventeenth Street, and Fourteenth Street in Sinkor. He left me and the kids in a rented house and built two houses for his girlfriend and her family. We lived together as husband and wife from 1972 to 1980 as renters, with no thoughts of putting my family in a home. With the help of God, who knew my heart very well, my desires came true. The One who answers all prayers allowed me to begin building a house for me and my children in December of 1983. I knew that I was 100 percent certain that God was saying yes in my situations. It shows in every instance or moment in your life at that time of trouble, because in the same way, he provided everything I needed. Mr. Steve Mellor,[3] who was one of the victims of the Lutheran church massacre, was my contracted engineer and builder. He did a good job for me. If you are completely sure of your decisions, remember you have God's blessing. *Go for it!*

Never allow anyone to bring you down or prevent you from experiencing what God has for you. Live a life with no regrets and no limits, no matter whatever circumstances life brings your way! God wants you to be extremely happy about life! Remember, we can do all things through Christ who gives us the strength. Finally, it was completed, and we moved into our house with much joy in 1985.

---

[3]   Mr. Steve Mellor died in July 1990.

Creating the Blueprint: My Storehouse

This was not just an ordinary house; it was what I dreamed of having. It had four bedrooms, a kitchen, two bathrooms, living and dining rooms, large front and back porches, and an extra bedroom for boys attached. After the first house, God didn't stop there. He also blessed us with another—a five-bedroom home. My God is a good God. He will not give you anything which is not good. He said in his Word, "Truly I tell you, whatever you bind on earth will be bound in heaven, and whatever you loose on earth will be loosed in heaven." Matthew 7:11 KJV says, "If ye then, being evil, know how to give good gifts unto your children, how much more shall your Father which is in heaven give good things to them that ask him?" Your God will give you the best—trust him!

It was the time to harvest all that I have sown. God is good! As Philippians 4:19 says, "My God will supply all my needs according to his riches in glory in Christ Jesus." Matthew 6:26 adds, "Look at the birds of the air, that they do not sow, nor reap nor gather into barns, and yet your heavenly Father feeds them. Are you not worth much more valuable?" Yes, you are, and I am!

My living room in Liberia

True Home Values

I was right there to see my eldest daughter Kosiapoe walked down the aisle. Out of this home came abundant joy.

I walked alongside the wedding vehicle from the Monrovia city hall
to my little home on Fourteenth Street where the reception was held.
There was a lot of joy running in my heart! (April 29, 1989)

MARTHA'S STORY

As a single mother, having a home for my children and I was fulfilling for me. I had values that were instilled in my home, no matter where I lived. I worked very hard to keep food on the table and every basic necessity of survival for my children. I started a little market to supplement my teacher's income from Calvary Baptist Elementary School. The system I had in place was an amazing tool in putting in the extra time and effort to build my own home and bringing joy to my children. At the same time, I was building a godly family. Taking my children to church and encouraging them to be engaged in a spiritual lifestyle was something I offered them also. My eldest daughter, Kosiapoe Mercy, had faith that was so strong during this season in serving the Lord as a young woman. Her lifestyle and upbringing was a blessing to me and everyone who came across her. This is a reward of training up a child in the way he or she should go: when he or she is old, he or she will not depart from it. Parents, never let your present condition limit the spiritual foundation you have to offer to your children.

My home was a resting place for so many people. Missionaries, pastors, and evangelists stayed in my home as they came to Monrovia for conferences, when visiting with their children, or when traveling to another county. My home was always open foraccommodations. They would pray with my children and me and always leave words of blessing.

Sometimes, some of them would bring food. The African culture is unique. When your guest is leaving, you would give them a souvenir. This makes them feel welcome. Family member and friends would send their children to me to attend school. The friends of the students would follow them home during school break time for vacations. The Lord provided means for me to always have enough to share with everyone. When you are building a home with a goal in mind, according to godly plans, you will end up with a finished product: a home that is structurally sound as well as aesthetically pleasing. Not unlike actual physical construction, building a godly home with God's kind of blueprint in mind creates a family that is strong and unbelievably fulfilling to be a part of. That's the home I had—a home full of love.

To those who may need advice in building a godly home, you must be confident in following God's plans. Then you will truly enjoy some great benefits along the way.

I was left to raise my daughters alone, all because they weren't the right gender. God saw all the ugliness underneath the facade and ordered my steps in spite of the trials.

What the scripture says concerning this matter, adultery:

- *Hebrew 13:4–5*. "Marriage should be honored by all, and the marriage bed kept pure, for God will judge the adulterer and all the sexually immoral. Keep your lives free from the love of money and be content with what you have, because God has said, 'Never will I leave you; never will I forsake you.'"
- *Romans 16:18*. "Anyone who divorces his wife and marries another woman commits adultery, and the man who marries a divorced woman commits adultery."
- *Matthew 5:27–28*. "You have heard that it was said, 'You shall not commit adultery.' But I tell you that anyone who looks at a woman lustfully has already committed adultery with her in his heart."

I am not a judge, but that is what the scripture says. I am very thankful to God for the path I chose—to commit my life to God and my four girls. Someone had to be the role model. They are a blessing to God first, then me, and Rufus, even though he didn't think anything good can come from a girl child. He disowned us in the eyes of man, himself, and God.

> Children are a heritage from the Lord, offspring a reward from him. Like arrows in the hands of a warrior are children born in one's youth. Blessed is the man whose quiver is full of them. They will not be put to shame when they contend with their opponents in court. (Psalm 127:3–5 NIV)

Here are the names of my girls, with their meaning in relation to my living.

- *Pastor Mercy K. Horace ("God's Mercy")*. The mercy of God kept us alive.
- *Bley J. Greaves ("God's Kindness")*. The kindness of God brought us through.
- *Dayanah B. Thomas ("Our Future")*. God had our future in his hand.
- *Degusia P. Soeh Mulbah ("Your Own")*. We are God's children. God is our owner.

God gives mercy to be kind to people. Look to the future, and know that God is and will always be our owner. .

I am grateful for the gift of the children he gave into my care. I was always offering my love to my children. I saw some things from my children's point of view, which helped me as well. I tried to be affectionate to my children, knowing what we were going through. I demonstrated the virtue of patience at all times to show them a good example. I knew my boundaries as they grew up as young women, and even as I went to visit each one of them in their adulthood, I knew my place as a mother. I prayerfully gave unconditional love to all my blood children, along with those who were adopted by me. I enjoyed having one-on-one time with each of my children. I never discussed my children's personal concerns with other person. None of them could change my principle concerning that. They all grew up learning that discipline—mostly gentle and nonviolent discipline—is a good thing. My children were my top priority: friends, neighbors, workmates, medical providers, and family members knew it, but I knew it the most. The greatest value in my home was rising up strong, self-assured, godly, and confident children. I was their mom, not their friend when growing up. Later, some became my friends. I was willing to get peed, pooped, and vomited on, and to work long night hours when it was needed. Having a sense of humor with my children was very important. I tried to have balance in my life because I wanted them to see the importance of having a balanced life in the midst of pain. Being strong enough to survive harsh conditions with a smile on my face was very important to me, and I believe they saw it. I was always proud of them when they did a good job at school while growing up, and even in their adulthood, they were acknowledged for good choices and better results.

Psalm 24:1 said, "The Earth is the Lord's and the fullness thereof."

No matter what we face in life, we must humble ourselves under the mighty hand of God. He will bring us through every challenge we face in life. First Peter 5:6–7 says "Humble yourselves therefore under the mighty hand of God that he may exalt us in due time. Because he cares we must cast our cares upon him for he careth for us."

In Psalm 30:56, David said, "Weeping may endure for a night but joy comes in the morning."

Before going on further, I have some songs I'd like to share! I am blessed; my God loves me. The Lord had been so good to me for me to be alive to write this story into a book today. It shows that I am blessed, and God has blessed me with life.

First Song
I am blessed, so blessed every day of my life
I am blessed when I wake up in the morning till I lay my head to rest
I am blessed, you are blessed, we are blessed

Second Song
My God loves me, his love will never end
He lives within my heart, for my God loves me
He loves you, he loves us

Third Song
They that wait on the Lord shall renew their strength
They shall mount up on wings as eagles
They shall run and not be weary
And shall walk and not faint
Teach me, Lord, how to wait, how to wait
[Isaiah 40:31]

Fourth Song
I don't know why Jesus loves me
I don't know why he came
I don't know why he sacrificed his life
Oh, but I am glad, I'm glad he did
(2X)

Fifth Song
Why worry when you can pray?
Trust Jesus, he'll be your stay
Don't be a doubting Thomas, rest fully on his promise
Why worry, worry when you can pray?

MARTHA ZEAH GARKPI

Leaning on God

Mom Transition moment Kosiapoe coming to USA

Final Days @ Living Word

Final days @ LWCCI

April 30, 2017 last outting with the Horace's on their
29, anniverary dinner before departure

MARTHA ZEAH GARKPI

I have always seen God's hands of mercy in my life so many times, and I know he is always near and with me. He is here in the good times and the bad times. He is here even when trouble rises. Trust him at his Word. In this moment of rejection from my husband, I knew to lean on God in spite of everything. *I knew I had to be still and know that he is God. I promise to exalt him among the nations. I will continue to exalt him in my lifetime. I was certain the plans he had for my life were plans for welfare and not for evil, to give me a future and a hope were his desires. All these marital challenges were just stepping-stones.*

Even though I was not treated the best and there was a degree of animosity that lingered, God healed me. This situation showed me that nothing keeps someone around unless they want to be kept. All my love and devotion was not enough. God's love was unfailing, though. I turned to him in prayer instead of choosing to be bitter about it. Being bitter gets you nowhere because you have no control over anyone's actions but your own.

Matthew 5:44–45 KJV says

> But I say unto you, love your enemies, bless them that curse you, do good to them that hate you, and pray for them which despitefully use you, and persecute you; That ye may be the children of your Father which is in heaven: for he maketh his sun to rise on the evil and on the good, and sendeth rain on the just and on the unjust.

In most societies where fathers are not present in their children's lives, it can be very difficult to find much joy in the heart of the children. With the help of the Lord, my children grew up with joy and contentment. I was blessed knowing that God was doing it for them. A wonderful father is one who is not only there financially, but is also there emotionally and spiritually for their children. My prayer for him is that God will make him a good and godly father. I pray that he realizes that children are a blessing from the Lord, not a burden, and that he also realizes that children are a parent's responsibilities. I pray not to forsake or leave my role as a mother for all their personal needs. I would have loved to see him there to help his children receive one of the best gifts a father can ever give to a child—that is to teach him or her to build a relationship with God. Fathers who are faithful to God will not mistreat their children. Rather, they will bring them up in a loving and caring environment.

God Can Change Your Life

Let me encourage all women with one gender of children: be happy. Why? Because they are a gift from God. He has a reason for them being here on earth. Being a single parent, I made lots of sacrifices that both parents should have made together. You can live a truly three-dimensional life if you look for harmony across each dimension of your relationship with your children, God, and yourself. I guarantee you, this will bring you joy alongside your daily trials and tribulations of parenting.

Mothers, be thankful for the fruit of your womb, whether they are a boy or girl. Bring your child up in the fear of the Lord, that they be God-fearing children. What man can't do, God can do for you. A male figure was not in my home to help bring up our children. It was challenging, but my God was there, and he is yet here right now.

In the story of Ruth, a foreigner provides a shining example of God's loving-kindness. After her Judean husband dies, Ruth leaves her home in Moab and travels back to Bethlehem with her mother-in-law, despite the prospects of poverty and insecurity that lay ahead of her. Ruth pledges loyalty to Naomi and her God. She works hard gleaning in the field to provide for herself and Naomi. (Potentially dangerous work, since she has no male protector.) God had a plan for the both of them. He also models integrity and loyalty, addressing the proper customs so that he can redeem this unusual family. Each of the key characters in this story (Ruth, Naomi, and Boaz) place the interests of the others ahead of their own, and thus they model Christ-like faith centuries before their descendant Jesus enters the scene. God will bring a fulfilling mate for you if it is in your desire to marry. He will help if it is in your desire to have children, just like he did for me. Enjoy every position you find yourself in in life because there is an end destination. Depending on how you live, it could be good or bad.

My four girls are all well-off, considering how we got here. They are all well-managed women today, and people look up to them. They're all married with children of their own. All four of them have boys and girls as children. They have loving, faithful, God-fearing husbands and live in good and peaceful homes, unlike the pain I endured. My eldest daughter, Pastor Mercy Horace, is pastoring right alongside her husband, Bishop Bedell Horace. And the rest of the girls are all in ministry, spreading the Word of God.

I can say that I am one happy woman. In fact, I am the happiest mother alive on earth. I pray to God to keep my children safe and close by him.

When you are deciding to make lifelong decisions, ask yourself:

- What am I looking for in a husband or wife?
- Is marriage what I really desire?
- What will I do in the case of divorce? Two wrongs can't make one right.
- How will I protect my marriage from predators?
- How will we maintain our commitment to our faith as a Christian husband and wife?

Keep these questions in mind.

God has his own way of bringing you out of a situation when you fully trust him. Nothing is too big or small for God to do. When I read these passages, it built my strength up in the Lord not to depend on my own knowledge, but fully on him. Can you please read with me? There is no way to conquer the enemy with the arms of the flesh. You cannot run from the devil no matter what he brings at you. Face it, as you depend on God for survival. Whether you change location or not, he can find you. I encourage you to stop running and face whatever is after you with the Word of God. Be reminded to say, it is written:

> Abram believed the LORD, and he credited it to him as righteousness.

> He also said to him, "I am the LORD, who brought you out of Ur of the Chaldeans to give you this land to take possession of it."

> But Abram said, "Sovereign LORD, how can I know that I will gain possession of it?"

> So the LORD said to him, "Bring me a heifer, a goat and a ram, each three years old, along with a dove and a young pigeon."

> Abram brought all these to him, cut them in two and arranged the halves opposite each other; the birds, however, he did not cut in half." (Genesis 15:6–10)

> Abram believed the LORD, and he credited it to him as righteousness.

> He also said to him, "I am the LORD, who brought you out of Ur of the Chaldeans to give you this land to take possession of it." (Genesis 3:6–7)

The Reason for My Life

What I know about God is this: he can change your rough life to a happy life. What a rough, hurtful, and painful life I went through. But through it all, God has always been there to soothe me where I hurt. There is a word from the Lord for everything that we go through in life. All you must do is believe and stand on his word and act on it.

Philippians 4:13 says, "I can do all things through Christ that strengthens me. I found my strength in looking unto Jesus the author and finisher of my faith."

Hebrews 13:6 says, "So that we may say boldly, the Lord is my helper, and I will not fear what man shall do unto me." Thank God for his Word.

He brought me through the civil war in my country. Let me tell you how. My coming through was rough, but it was by the power of his might. I made a promise to my God in this lifetime that I will surrender my all to him. I will continue to give God all the praises due to his faithfulness to my children and me.

Because we are human beings, we sin. When I think of the goodness of God and see all he had in store for me, all I want to do is praise him. He is worthy to be praised.

God has so many times saved me from natural and spiritual death. He kept me safe from evildoers, and he will do it for you too, if you trust him for all in all your ways.

What seems good to the eyes is not always good. See through the eyes of God and study to know his Word. Touch not those things forbidden by God.

Fight the good fight of faith! Stay with God no matter what you face in life. With God you will come out the winner!

CHAPTER FOUR

Walking in the Shadow of Death

History of the Liberian Civil War

I WAS BORN and raised in Liberia. I immigrated to the United States in December 2000 and became a citizen after spending several years as a refugee in Ivory Coast and Ghana as a result of a devastating civil war in my country of birth. I could not imagine any sight of this horror coming into our beloved country, Liberia. It took the blood of Jesus to filter these horrific memories away.

Liberia is a unique country. Its history is a history of American and African slavery bundled together.

Liberia was founded in 1822 as an outpost for returning freed slaves from the Americas. It grew into a colony and eventually became a commonwealth, and achieved independence in 1847 with the help of the American Colonization Society, a private organization made mainly of slaveholders in the United States. It was governed by white agents of the society until 1841, when the first Negro vice governor of the Commonwealth of Liberia, Joseph Jenkins Roberts, became its leader on the death of the white governor, Thomas Buchanan.

On July 26, 1847, Liberia declared independence and became the first independent republic on the African continent. It adopted all the social and political traditions of the United States and tailored its constitution along the lines of the United States of America. The new land was already inhabited by native tribes, who vastly outnumbered the African Americans. Much like European settlers elsewhere in Africa, the colonists saw themselves as bringing civilization, Christianity, and commerce to the unenlightened Africans. The history of Liberia is rife with the segregation between the sons and daughters of freed slaves on one hand and those of the native inhabitants of the land.

Descendants of the freed slaves, generally known as Americo-Liberians, remained in social and political control of the country and ensured economic and social advancements among themselves against the native descendants. This condition eventually led to civil unrest in 1979 and the violent overthrow of the settler government in a coup d'état on April 12, 1980. For the first time, a son of native descent, Samuel K. Doe, assumed power. He presided over a new system of repression against descendants of the settlers and children of other native groups, Gios and Manos. Due to some unresolved conflict, tension started building up. This conflict would eventually lead to a civil war that destroyed what little had been built over 160 years of Liberian history.

The Liberian Civil War was one of Africa's bloodiest civil wars in my era. At the time, the population was a strong 2.1 million. These wars took more than two hundred thousand Liberian lives and displaced a million other citizens in refugee camps in neighboring countries.

In the early 90's, the Economic Community of West African States (ECOWAS) entered Monrovia. They became the peacekeepers.

After the death of the president, an interim government was formed, and Dr. Sawyer became the nation's president. The fighting continued because other leaders did not want to work with the interim government. This caused a major disruption in the push for peace.

The fighting became so intense that more civilian casualties occurred as a result. In 1992, there was also an attack on Monrovia called Operation Octopus. Many lives were lost after this as well. According to sources, they all agreed to disarm themselves and abide by UN-monitored elections in 1997. After the election, Mr. Taylor became the president, and he ruled all of Liberia.

The Lutheran Church Massacre

The above stories from the writers state the position we were in as common citizens. We were displaced, leaving everything behind and running for our lives. Where we went and where was safe was a major concern. These forces were fighting a meaningless war. They could not see their enemy, and we got caught in the middle of an endless battle. The lack of running water and the shortage of food supplies left us eating green leaves, if any could be found. The healthcare system, the educational system, and all other major infrastructures collapsed. We all asked each other daily "What will happen to us—the nation of Liberia and the next generation to come?" "What have we gotten ourselves into?" "How long will this go on?" Only God knew.

Thank God for securing our lives as he did. It's his grace and mercy covering us that keeps us alive still today. God is an awesome protector!

We lived in fear, because in war you don't know if you will make it out or not. We sat with anxiety, waiting at this church in the hope of peace. One day, a great attack came upon us by some soldiers. It was very sad because no matter what force won, we the Liberian people would lose.

We all were settling down for the night on Sunday, July 29, 1990. We heard the arrival of large vehicles and the sound of a crowd of people with terrified voices. A soldier said, "Gentlemen, turn off the lights. We will finish them up tonight. Do not use the gun. Don't use all of the bullets. Use the knives, cutlasses, and swords." Oh my god! The night was very long, lying right beside them and not being able to speak. The only thing that separated us was the front door to the church. When my granddaughter was about to cry, I asked my daughter Blessing to breastfeed the child. The night became horrifying with the intensifying voices of the people at the Lutheran church crying out for their lives.

The people were screaming as the soldiers were using every weapon they had to destroy lives. Guns were shooting; people were jumping through windows to escape. It was horrible. This was a terrible time for us. Within our building, we had people coming around warning us to keep it real quiet and completely silent because of what was going on. They did not want any attention drawn to the building. It would be even worse because it wasn't the only edifice at the Lutheran church. This nightmare went on until about 5:00 a.m.

By this time, those who were upstairs on the second floor of the Lutheran church school facility were being visited by vigilant soldiers. No one was shot in the seventh and eighth-grade classrooms. The seventh was the particular room we were in before taking my grandbaby for medication, where we were not allowed back in. They shouted at the ceiling and asked the residents for money and valuables. In the room were my daughter Blessing; granddaughter Love; Angela and her daughter TeTe; Menka, Blessing's adopted daughter; not forgetting Blessing's play daughter, the late Monwonser K.; and a host of friends and family members. We lived at that facility for 2½ months. Three days before this attack, my granddaughter got so sick, and we had to take her from there to find medication. Upon our return to the Saint Peter's Lutheran Church Compound, where we had taken refuge, we were told not to enter. According to them, we were told not to leave the compound, and we did, so for that reason, wewere not allowed entrance. No answer we gave was sufficient. They continued to say, "Go back where you came from." These were their instructions. Not knowing or realizing that it was God speaking for us not to enter, it was a scary moment at the time. *Where do we go from here? Home on Fourteenth Street? Where do we go?* We were not safe at home by ourselves. Our tribe was being hunted from home to home to get rid of us. Most of my family members were there with their kids, as well as my church members and friends. The only decision was to go across the street from the Lutheran church to the Methodist church, which was not safe. It was a standalone building, not fenced in. We had no choice but to run to the church very fast. The location was directly facing the Saint Peter's Lutheran Church, which was on the opposite side of the church. It was very packed too with the Gio and Mano tribes. We had no choice but to go and ask for shelter at the United Methodist Church. There was no more space anywhere in the building. The only spot available was located at the immediate entrance of the facility. As a description, when you enter the church, the foyer of the edifice is right at the immediate opening.

Within days of being at the Methodist shelter, the most horrific thing that the human race could ever imagine happened. Nonstop killing! Our sleeping location was right at the entrance of that church. We could hear people screaming for their lives, growling like dogs. My seven-month-old grandchild wanted to cry. We asked God to calm her down. The least noise that could have been heard would have drawn attention to all of us at the Methodist church.

God's Hedge of Protection

God's Word says, "When the wicked, even mine enemies and my foes, came upon me to eat up my flesh, they stumbled and fell." We had to put on the full armor of God daily so that we could stand against the devil's schemes. We knew that God was our hiding place. He will protect us from trouble and surround us with songs of deliverance.

God is our refuge and strength, an ever-present help in trouble. Every moment we needed him, we were confident that he would come as our helper; for that reason, we were not afraid. Daily, we recited, "No weapon formed against us will prosper." We stood on it as our heritage being children of God.

The morning of July 30, 1999, the remaining survivors ran from the Lutheran church along with the remaining from the Methodist church. Where could we go from there? The vigilant killers, our own soldiers, were all driving up and down the city streets, looking for "rebels" to get rid of. God used our men to direct us to the USAID compound along the boulevard, where we were instructed to go take refuge away from our own government. At this time, we joined the rest of the people who survived the Lutheran church attack in marching to the USAID's compound. I took along with me two children whose mother died at the Lutheran church. I asked for Monwonser.

TeTe, Angeline's[4] daughter, replied, "She left the room to get some money from her mother who was in the school auditorium."

"Why?" I replied.

"When the soldier entered the room, he screamed at everyone to give money for their life, and everyone began digging in their purses and bags. It was at this time Monwonser K. left the room to get her money from her mom in the auditorium."

She didn't know what was going on outside. According to TeTe, when they were coming out the morning of the killing, they found her body. How sad! It broke our hearts, especially Blessing's. Monwonser[5] only came in the room because of her play mom, who was my daughter Blessing. They both loved each other and always wanted to be together. May her dear soul rest in peace!

We arrived at this compound in a large group, trembling and clueless of what to do next. Within forty-five minutes, we found ourselves surrounded by the government troops calling on us to come out of the compound or else we would be burned in the compound. I thought we were in the right place for protection, but no! The enemy was raging with some uncontrolled anger and blood thirstiness. USAID, being the lead US government agency that works to end extreme global poverty and enable resilient, democratic societies to realize their potential, was supposed to protect us. Instead, they were afraid, and they turned us over to those blood thirsty people. Was their property more important than our lives? No, but human nature seeks to look out for oneself.

---

[4]   Angeline went home to be with the Lord in 2015.

[5]   Monwonser K. went home to be with the Lord July 1990.

During the stay at the Lutheran church, we were guided each night by USAID personnel along with their dogs. They never came back to check on us after we arrived in the compound.

The USAID staff asked us to leave the compound. They stated that they did not want any trouble from the Liberian government. I still feel disappointed to this day. That was not the right decision, knowing what they claimed to stand for in any given country is to be of some protection or a voice. Rather, their lives and property were more important than the people they came in the country for.

We are back in the street of Sinkor once more, running here and there like chickens that had just been loosed from the coop. The soldiers then opened fire on us! We all ran in different directions. But praise be unto God that he kept me and my children together, along with the two children. Dead bodies were all around and about us, a horrible sight to imagine in a country that you call your homeland. Liberia was no longer a peaceful place, but God kept us in his divine plan. What a great blessing indeed! Only God did it for us. We were not far from where we used to live, so we ran into that direction. People that were not of the Gio and Mano tribes were in a shack, watching us run in the street while being shot at. Unimaginable! We were legitimate citizens of Liberia. We should not have gone through their power struggle! At this point, I praised God I separated my family. Emmanuel D., Judy, Dayanah, Degusia, the late Sam Demey's two boys, Joseph K., the late Sangar's son, Emmanuel S. were sent to the late Counselor Smallwood's farm on Bong Mines Road. Yekakpah W. was sent to Nimbi. I spread my kids around for survival. It was hard, but it had to be done.

Blessing, Love, Menka Grace's foster daughter, Anthony K., my nephew, along with my play daughter, the late *Angeline, and her daughter TeTe were left in Monrovia at the time of the war. Of course, we were in our own country with host of relatives and family members from all over, from Monrovia to the surrounding cities of Liberia.

MARTHA ZEAH GARKPI

God took us to our house on Fourteenth Street, along the avenue where one of the party headquarters was. Among those who followed me for survival was pastor John W., Abraham M., and Nixon Z. We were not allowed to reenter our own home. We were now considered rebels because we were of the Gio ethnic tribe. However, there was a man by the name of Mr. Onie, who worked with my daughter Blessing at LEC. He gave us the authorization to reenter.

He said, "Gentlemen, leave them alone. She worked for the Liberian government. She is one of us, even though she is from the tribe we are hunting for. Let's leave them alone and keep watch on them, please."

The morning of July 31, we entered our own home again, with the fearful feeling of the unknown. We were now surrounded with no one else but us. My boys who escaped from the Lutheran church came looking, and they knew we were at home. They joined us—Anthony K., my nephew, and the above named.

On August 2, 1990, we experienced another deadly episode. It was around 10:30 p.m. when the death squad of the ruling government came at our residence. They began beating and kicking at the door. "Let us in! You are rebels. You have to die. You must die!" During this time, there was a young soldier on guard between the NDPL headquarters and our residence. He ran and called out for Mr. Onie, and according to him, he said, "Come quick! One of our death squads is at the door of the family you asked us to protect."

Can you imagine the terror we went through at this moment? We had four young men in the house, along with us three ladies and three children. We began to pray and call on God.

During the prayer, we heard Mr. Onie say, "Gentlemen, please don't kill them! Please, not tonight! Not on my watch! Please, gentlemen, please! Not them. . . please!" As we heard Mr. Onie from outside, we were paralyzed with fear because he was pleading on our behalf. He called to us inside the house. "Mother and Ms. Blessing, open the door. It is me, Onie."

The boys went into the attic of the house for safety, and my girls held each other as I walked toward the door. I knew if God did not come through for us, then it was our time. I was saying the Twenty-Third Psalm as I walked toward the door to open it. When I opened the door, I held onto Mr. Onie very tight. He was one of their commanding generals. He said, "It is okay."

They entered our house, hollering and holding us at gunpoint. They asked us what our tribe was, and we replied that we are Gio. "That's good. You people are the ones we are looking for."

The death squad called out, "We smelled men. Where are they? If you do not produce them, we will start shooting."

I cried out to my boys to come out from the attic, and they came down. All the food we had purchased for survival was all hauled out by my boys into the army vehicles. We were ordered to give up all of our foodstuff. But praise be to God that he shut the mouth of the hungry, bloodthirsty lion, and our lives were spared that night through a vessel that knew my daughter from work. God will continue to do what he says he will do. We can say as Daniel did in Daniel 6:21:

> Daniel answered, "May the king live forever! My God sent his angel and he shut the mouths of the lions. They have not hurt me, because I was found innocent in his sight. Nor have I ever done any wrong before you, Your Majesty."

The next morning of August 3, 1990, we sat and felt so hopeless. *What next, Lord?* I prayed with the four boys and sent them away with hope that we will meet again one day. It was not long before we had another soldier who came to our house. I believe he came around, and perhaps he may have heard what the death squad did to us the night before.

He said, "My name is Kollie. I live on Twelfth Street. Leave everything behind and follow me to my house. Everyone will not die."

God rescued us again! The night before, the friendly soldier Mr. Onie told the squad not to kill us, but to leave us until the next day.

The Valley

We picked up and followed this friendly soldier, Kollie, who took us to his house where we stayed for eight days. He showed kindness to us, including providing security, food, and shelter. He told the people in the community that we were his family. He was of the Kpelle/Loma ethnic group. For this reason, the people were kind to us. We all lived there happily for eight days, until the night of August 11, 1990, when everything changed. He had come home from a "mission," as they call it, from attacking the wounded survivors at the John F. Kennedy Hospital. He bragged about it as he came in the door. His appearance and behavior this time was not too pleasant.

He said "Hey, let's go outside." We asked what for. "I will kill you tonight because you are rebels." He held us at gunpoint and called us rebels. He had blood all over him, and he was speaking, saying, "All that I am doing, one day I will be killed, and you will stay alive. For this reason, I will kill you before I die."

We lived in a rental house, so when he was screaming, the other renters and the landlord were awakened by the noise.

The landlord began to beg on our behalf. "Please don't kill them! These people are your own people. Maybe you aren't okay right now, but please don't kill them."

From all the noise around him of the begging and pleading, he got confused. Life had already left me. I remember my daughter Blessing right on my side along with my granddaughters, my play daughter, and her daughter, TeTe. We were praying out loud when all the noise was going on around us. We kept calling on the name of Jesus. He heard us. God listens to his people all the time. In Psalm 34:15b, "He hears their cry for help," David tells us. He hears their petitions, and he understands their needs before they ask. Psalm 34:17b says the righteous cry out, and the LORD hears and delivers them out of all their troubles. God communicates to people through his words and in actions.

After a while, he said, "It is okay. You go to bed."

It was almost 11:00 p.m. All we heard was a sound of someone jumping down from a window. Immediately, the five of us ran into our home. We headed out the back door into that deep darkness that was curfew time. The very first house we arrived at, we knocked for help. All we heard was "Who is it?" and we said, "It's us." The door opened, and we saw no one at that moment. We don't know whose house it was, nor what danger we were heading into. We weren't concerned about it. We got out in faith, and we were walking in faith. We all wondered who opened the door. As we walked into the house, we saw an older woman and her husband sitting on their bed, on opposite sides, praying.

They asked us, "How did you get in?"

We replied, "You opened the door."

At this point, they became afraid of us and were very quiet. They sat up looking at us as we looked at them.

In no time, we heard on the outside, "Kollie, we thought you said you just had some rebels. Where are they?"

We heard him saying, "This way, quickly!"

MARTHA ZEAH GARKPI

"Where did they go?"

"I left them in the house."

Someone said, "There is no way these people will get out in such darkness."

"No, I am not lying. I had some rebels," Kollie said.

"You lied to us! We will kill you, Kollie! If you don't produce these people by tomorrow, it won't be nice for you."

He said, "We will put out a search for them tomorrow. There is no way they can leave this area. They are very afraid."

They looked all over. We, as well as the older couple, were listening. Amazingly, God shut their mouth from calling out to the crew. No one said a word in this horrifying moment. Blessing continued to breastfeed her baby in this whole ordeal, in hopes that Love wouldn't cry. Back then Love was an understanding child. As a baby, Love had so many encounters that saved our lives. Her illness took us from the Lutheran church. Just before at the Liberia and Ivory Coast border, we were arrested by some of the Liberian military border patrol. They were trying to prevent us from leaving the country. This was very intense, and God used Love again divinely to bring us out. Love is a prophetic child—my divine grandchild. Please keep her, Lord!

This miracle was a great deliverance for us. When morning came, Blessing left the house with such courage to seek a means of an escape for us. I knew that God would provide a means of other miraculous sources. However, the journey and the direction in which she headed was very frightening for me as her mother. We prayed, and she left. By 9:00 a.m., the older couple left the house.

As they were leaving, they said, "When your daughter comes back, you can stay in the house. We are moving across the bridge to our children. We won't say a word about what happened last night. May God protect you."

The house remained still until Blessing's return. No one knew we were there, and it needed to stay that way. The Lord provided a means of deliverance by the divine leading of my daughter Blessing. That is her testimony. If you have an opportunity, contact her, and she will best narrate it.

She finally came back at about 1:30 p.m., and we all began to rush to get away from the scene. We knew what was coming, and we didn't want anything to do with it. The whole departure process was being played by the Lord Jesus and a host of many angels. Oh, what a moment of joy, fear, and troubling spirit! We drove from Twelfth Street and arrived at Maturity Center at the intersection of Jallah Town and Somalia Drive (Capitol Bypass). There was a major checkpoint here. We were caught and recognized as rebels. We were asked to get out of the car to be killed. After many confrontations between the driver (who just so happened to be a soldier of high standing) and the government soldiers, known as the death squad, we knew that only God could save us. If not, that was it.

Immediately, God sent a ram in the bush. Suddenly, someone yelled out "Oh, that is Jacob N.!" Everyone's attention went to him and his vehicle. In this breathtaking moment, by the orchestration of God, the driver took off in the vehicle, initiating a high-speed chase.

From that point, our guardian angel drove past the military barracks, and we were dropped off at the Antoinette Tubman Stadium. He began crying out, "Gentlemen, don't open fire on them! Let these ones live!" At this point, he knew immediately that we were of the Gio tribe. We began running for our lives. Blessing ran back to hug him, and I heard him say, "*Go! Go!* Don't look back!"

This deliverance was just as it was for the Israelites. God had to have opened his eyes for that intervention to take place. He was instructed to take us back to the army barracks, according to Blessing. But God rescued us in such an awesome way. In the midst of all the turmoil, I began to pray. "Lord, please let us live!" This point was a point of no escape. The boundaries were between the Doe government soldiers and the NPFL group on the intersection of Lynch Street and Sekou Toure Avenue.

Oh what a story to tell! I am speechless for God to have used my Blessing to bring us to safety. This is a lifelong story that will never be forgotten. I told her I owed my life to her for saving me. She will laugh; she is such a brave young lady. She believes that she can do all things through Christ that lives in her. I always reminded her, "Mama, your mission is not over yet!" Our goal was to go and find my children, her sisters, and the other children. We all were separated for survival purposes. In a place that we were unable to freely walk because of our ethnic background, God brought us there in less than hour. This is how we entered the rebel's terrain. August 17, 1990, was a day to remember, where we now could have a normal life in this location (Douala).

While in Douala, one of the renters from the house that we almost died in, by the hands of Kollie, greeted us. She was so happy to see us. She said, "Guess what? The next day some big, big soldiers came asking us whether we saw some strange people that did not belong in the neighborhood. 'They are supposed to be rebels, and we are in search of their whereabouts.' We said that we had no idea. We were all threatened. They took Kollie away, and he never came back. We believe they killed him. But anyway, what is your tribe?"

Blessing said, "We are Kpelle."

"Oh! What's wrong with that man? Why did he want you all to die for nothing?"

We did not say any more words, and we separated from her presence. Now Kollie, who had been our helper, providing food and shelter for us, planned an evil plot against us. We think he did it because it was said that whenever you produce a rebel, they give you a higher rank. God turned our enemy into a footstool, and now we were somehow free from the fiery furnace. It was disappointing, because he was nice to us. How sad that all the people we thought were good had an evil intention. "One who plans to do evil, men will call a schemer" (Proverbs 24:8).

Psalm 140:2 says, "Who devise evil things in their hearts; they continually stir up wars." Psalm 21:11–11 adds, "Though they intended evil against you and devised a plot, they will not succeed."

Let's look now behind NPFL lines. While at Douala, things were not conducive for us; the battle was still hot. Rockets were flying all around us. I was still not feeling fine or secure. Even while the peacekeeping force was on the ground, rockets were still flying over the country. I was trying to decide what to do. My children were scattered all around. Some went north, and some went west. We had no transportation and had to walk through jungle and brush no matter what direction we went. This prompted the move we made to VOA Number 10 building. While in Douala, we came across one of my dear sisters, Martha D., and my brother Sam Demey.[6] We were able to travel with the both of them from Prince J. Zone to Charles T. Zone.

The journey Blessing took to go rescue Brother Sam and Sister Martha's son, Nathan B., was a mission. Please ask Blessing because that was another impossible mission. They arrived almost 9:00 p.m. that night, and we were awestruck. They walked from Douala to Ricks Institute Building, and we started our journey to Bong Mines the next morning.

Journey of Faith

It was now August 24, 1990. We have been at the VOA Number 10 Building for a week now. We knew it wouldn't be permanent, as our lives were still in grave danger because of the intertribal connection

---

[6]   Sam Demey—may his soul rest in peace.

we have. While we were at the VOA Building, the peacekeeping force and rebels starting fighting, and again we were forced to uproot. On September 8, 1990, we left the VOA Number 10 Building and went to the Ricks Institute campus.

Something strange happened before we left. The late president Samuel K. Doe was assassinated on September 9, 1990. Sorrow gripped my heart. He was the president, and it was sad for his life to end that way. The next day, there was a heavy-duty rocket attack on the VOA. We then departed and headed for safety again.

Now at the Ricks Institute, we stayed only a few days because there was serious fighting going on between the NPFL and the ECOMOG soldiers over the hydro plant. We had an urge within our spirit to keep moving on. We left the Ricks on September 17, 1990, and headed for Suehn Mission, where we resided up to October 6, 1990. We then headed for Todee in Maigibi County. While traveling to Todee, there were several attacks made on us. Walking through the forested roads, we crossed one island then another. The third island we came across, we weren't so lucky. We fell into an ambush set by the NPFL.

There, we were questioned and threatened. We were even told by the commander CBR at this place that we should go back to where we came from. But after having narrated all of the things that had happened to us, especially at the Lutheran church, he became sympathetic. He then ordered someone to sing a song of captivity. They chanted, cursing the late President Doe's mother. I don't know if that was a way of making themselves feels better, they did it anyway. We had no idea. He then became friendly and lodged us for a day. The next day, he escorted us to Todee.

We stayed three days at Todee. While sitting quietly one morning, a soldier came and asked me what was wrong with me. I told him I was thinking about my children. Right then, one other soldier said to me that I resembled someone he knew. I became afraid because whenever a soldier said you looked like someone they knew, it was the end of your life. They will kill you because you are not their friend. So I said, "No, I look like myself."

So he said, "You look like someone I know in Todee, from a farm owned by one Mr. Smallwood. The person's name is . . . Bley!"

Then I said, "Oh yes! She is my daughter!"

I was beyond ecstatic! The Lord answered my prayers. Not knowing where we were going, or the land we were traveling, we managed to find another guardian angel. God said that he would show us great and mighty things, and this was nothing but his grace and mercy being shown to us. The commander for this area who had escorted us asked him to take us to the farm since he knew the children.

So we left Todee to go to Mr. Smallwood's[7] farm. Passing through the bush from 6:00 a.m. to 9:00 p.m., we finally reached the farm. By the time we reached the farm, some of the children had already left from the farm and went to Bong Mines. That night we thanked Mr. Smallwood for taking care of my children. Then he began to tell us a story about what my children did for him too. Counselor Smallwood was a wonderful man whom God brought into the lives of my children and me. He helped me through the chaos with my ex-husband. He became another shoulder to cry on, and through his intervention, by agreeing to take my and other people's children; they were able to survive all the tragedy in Monrovia. I trusted them in his care. May his soul rest in peace!

God passed through him to save my children when the war was really hot. After the children had stayed on the farm a few days, according to him, the NPFL soldiers came on the farm. Upon their arrival, they arrested Mr. Smallwood on the farm. Their charges were lodging soldiers and being in possession of guns. He said all this was not true,

---

[7]   Counselor Ephraim Smallwood went home to the Lord October 25, 1999.

as he was a lawyer with an abundance of farms. After nullifying the accusations against him, they finally decided to take him away for more questioning. However, as they were carrying him off, all of the children started crying for him. Some even began to speak Gio.

The NPFL soldiers realized where they were from and still wanted to investigate Mr. Smallwood further for even keeping the Gio children on his farm. The soldiers then decided to take the children along with them. They were puzzled as to how he ended up with the children in the first place. The kids went with him to the Bong Mines and later to Kakata.

As God could or would have it, he and all the children were relieved and brought back safely to his farm. All accusations against him were dropped. He said to me, "Thank God to you for your children. They were a help and blessing to me also." After a few days on the farm, I thanked him, and we left for Bong Mines to meet the friendly NPFC soldier who had already carried some of my children there, giving them food and good treatment.

We are a family again. Despite all the obstacles, we were reunited. It was now October 15, 1990. We had been in Bong Mines for three days now. I became homesick for our suburban life in Tappita Nimba County, away from the constant paranoia and ruckus. Remembering our tribal interconnection, I knew that that was not an option. My family and I were no longer secure in this country.

As I thought on this, an old friend by the name of Ms. E came to where we were and relayed to the soldier we were staying with that we were Krahn people. "What are you doing with them?" The fellow became concerned about our life and made his own decision of taking us to the Ivory Coast instead of taking us to Tappita. After a deep observation, he knew we were not safe anywhere in Liberia at this time. My life had been threatened on both sides, but God! It was threatened by Doe's soldiers because I am a Gio woman who once married a Krahn man.

He acted as if he didn't care to protect us from the Krahn soldiers. I was threatened again by those on the rebel line. Now here I am again, fearful and confused because my life isn't safe anymore in Liberia.

We left Bong Mines on November 2, 1990, for Danana, but there were several attempts on our lives while traveling. Our friend, this freedom fighter by the name of George, constantly pleaded on our behalf as we traveled. With the help of God, we arrived in Danana, and we were very excited that we were together once again as a family. We were in a strange country where we have never traveled before, but we knew that God was working it out for our good. Where do we go now? Our soldier friends that escorted us to the Ivory Coast recommended us to an Ivorian family that they knew. They were generous enough to take us in.

My children and I, therefore, waited in Danana. It was a safe haven for us. We waited for God to give us further directives about where we should lay our heads to take a rest and build our nest. Our first place came around November 5, 1990, when we made a stop in Mulubadukue. We resided at Mr. and Mrs. Paska's home.

While in Danana, my children and I faced some difficult times. Kosiapoe sold things at the market to meet other needs we had and to add to the food donations we were receiving. We joined the refugee family to work on a farm that was given to the Liberian refugees by UNICEF. Our labor on the farm helped to bring in other supplements for us. We produced lots of vegetables and raised a lot of cattle. Items from the farm were distributed among us, and some were sold to keep the home going. We were a part of a fellowship that was established by some Liberians. There was so much love in our community it made us forget that we were displaced at some time. The name of our church was Liberian Refugee Fellowship, with Brother Patrick Nuahn and Sister Nuahn as our pastors. They were great leaders.

My children and I worked along with the church for 2½ years. I served as the women's fellowship leader, and my children sang in the choir, taught Sunday school, and worked with the youth group before we left for Ghana.

We spent two months and went down to Nyingle, where we found a house to rent. Our landlord, Gua Francisua, had two wives, which was the Nyingle culture. They both were very kind to us.

We stayed there four months in Danana, and the Lord opened a door for my eldest daughter to join her husband Pastor Bedell Horace in the USA in April 1991. By the grace of God, they worked hard together to take care of us in Africa.

Discerning Spirit

In this story, I am about to reveal to you a lesson I learned while in Danana in 1992. It was yet another escape from death.

In life, I had heard people say that people have killed others using witchcraft. I didn't believe it until it happened in front of my eyes.

While in Danana, there was a lady from Upper Nimba, Liberia, who was a friend of our landlord. One night, a girl by the name of Bee came calling on me at my house. We were all asleep at the time, and she knocked on the window to wake us up.

She told me, "Ma, my mother needs you! Please come with me."

I asked, "At this time of night?"

She said, "Please!"

I woke up one of my boys and told him that Bee's mother called upon me. I went, and when I got to her house, she had her baby on her back and was pacing frantically.

"What happened?"

She told me, "Something is bothering me."

I asked her, "What?"

She remained silent. She just kept pacing!

Her daughter then said, "You sent me to call the lady, so please tell her why you called her here!"

She began to tell me. First she said, "Martha, be very careful with people. What I am about to tell you is about life and death." She continued, "One lady in this place, she's my best friend. But she doesn't like you or your children."

I asked, "Why?"

"It's because everybody in this place likes or loves you and your kids in so many ways. Your girls aren't like the other girls here. Plus you and your daughters are loved by landlord and his wife. Isn't that something how people don't like you because you put God first and his righteousness?"

She then told how that woman had wanted her to poison me. How evil! She said, "When you died, she had plans to harm your children!"

When she told me this, I was in disbelief.

She said, "It is the truth." She said she told her no. "My spirit had been bothering me. I can't eat, and I can't sleep! If I do this wickedness, how will I be able to look in your children's faces? We all escaped from the war and death, and then I am going to come and kill you?"

I replied, "For real?"

"No, I can't do that!" she said. "I am telling you to do something about it! But know how to go about it. Whenever you ask her about it, and she lies, you can call on me to testify for you."

Micah 2:1 (KJV) says, "Woe to those who scheme iniquity, who work out evil on their beds, when morning comes, they do it, for it is in the power of their hands." These people give themselves to be used by the devil. They are his agents. Look out for Satan's people. They live in our neighborhoods; go to church with us—some are in our very own family. They are in our jobs, and so forth. We encounter them daily in the various places that we go. Cover yourself with the blood of Jesus.

According to the confider, this lady who wanted me dead had asked her to do this three times. "She wants me to do her killing for her."

After that they took me back home. Can you believe this? It's mind-blowing! When I got home, I sat with my children. I could not sleep, so I woke my son-in-law Larry Taylor up and told him the story. He said, "Let's pray about it, because this is unbelievable."

I began to meditate on God's Word again. This is all that I have as a strong support. I said to myself, "Am I alive, or what?" I went to God and began to focus on these scriptures:

> You have seen all their vengeance, all their schemes against me. You have heard their reproach, O LORD, All their schemes against me. (Lamentations 3:60–61)

Suddenly, I heard a noise at the back of the building. To my amazement, it was a cow hitting the house on the very side where my bed was. The cow was hitting it so hard I began to hit the wall back from within. The cow stopped hitting the wall. I prayed and went back to sleep.

In my sleep, I found myself dreaming. I was dreaming that I was sitting down. I saw a cow walking toward me, and it looked at me. The cow looked like half woman and half man. The cow talked to me like he was a real person.

The cow said to me, "I am here for us to fight." Then, he tried to impale me with his horns. All of a sudden, the cow dropped dead!

I fell into deep sleep and had another dream. I went to buy food, and I saw this lady talking to her friend. "Why don't you want to do what I asked you to do? Please do it for me, please?" Her friend shouted back, "No! *No!*" Then I woke up in a panic, not knowing if it was day or night.

One of my girls said, "A cow been here last night. It pooped in one of the neighbor's yards."

I then explained to my girls what the lady had told me yesterday. I also told them about the dream I had just had.

They said, "We are going to ask her about that right now!"

I told them, "Not yet."

While we were talking, the evil woman's landlord came by the house to buy some rice and bread. We told him about what we have been told; however, we did not call the lady's name. He told us that we should tell our landlord about the visit and the dream. We sent for him.

When he did come, we explained to him the dream. He told us to get to the zone chief, along with the refuge head, and tell them about the dream. I took two of my girls, and we went about our way. When we arrived there, I told him about the dream.

After I had explained the dream to him, he interpreted it to me. The first thing he did was call me by my birth name, "Zeah." He asked if this was my name.

I said, "Of course! That is my name."

MARTHA ZEAH GARKPI

Then he said, "The dream you had is a real thing going on in your life now." He told his wife, "This lady sitting before me, her name is Zeah." She came. "She has her children with her."

His wife said, "God is really with her."

He said, "Look, I don't know you from anywhere. This is my first time seeing and talking to you, but what you are telling me through your dream is not a dream."

I asked, "Why?"

"The woman you are telling us about is always here talking about you."

He said, for some odd reason, "I do not need a decision now, but what do you want me to do? I am the government's eyes, as well as our society's eyes. I am so happy that you were notified about it. In which way do you want to me to call her on it?"

I said, "We need to ask her, and this needs to be heard in a court setting. Call her in. You could ask her."

So he did send for her to come, and he sent for my church family and my children. We all went to court, and the judge found her guilty. People begged for her for the first time, so the justice of peace ordered her not to come my way or mention my name anywhere again.

Immediately I began to meditate on Psalm 27:2–3. "When the wicked, even mine enemies and my foes, came upon me to eat up my flesh, they stumbled and fell." Every plan she had planned was crumbling down through dreams and revelations. "Though a host should encamp against me, my heart shall not fear: though war should rise against me, in this will I be confident." I was not afraid because no weapon formed against me will prosper!

Guess what happened next? She went to my brother, whom she did not know was family, and told him what she was going to do to one lady by the name of Zeah. She just wouldn't quit! We went back to court, and this time, I revealed how I had found out about her plot. Of course, she denied everything.

So now, the court asked me to bring forth the lady who had revealed the news to me. The lady herself was not there, but her daughter was. That morning they came and called for me to come to court.

Before the girl could come to the court, the witch lady said, "If any lady comes and says that I even went over to her house and that I called Zeah's name, then I am guilty. I never asked anyone to do any killing for me." She was lying to them in my face!

Suddenly, Bee came, and she looked at the lady face-to-face and said, "I will wait until my mother could come, but if anything, I will let you know when she arrives."

The judge said, "Okay, Bee, before you go back home, this is a life-and-death matter. Since you are waiting for your mother, from today's date you are responsible for their family's life until your mother can come."

Surely, the Lord God does nothing unless he reveals his secret counsel to his servants. If this matter was not known to God, it would not have been revealed to me. The purpose and the plan of God would not have been fulfilled. I am very grateful to God for my life and the purpose he has for me!

The justice of peace told Bee, "The government's eyes are on you because you were the one who went to this lady's house at night to get her in order for all this information to be revealed to her. Is that true?" Bee answered yes. Right then, she put up her hand and said she swore to tell the truth, and she took the stand. She relayed the story as best as she heard it.

MARTHA ZEAH GARKPI

Lamentations 3:62 says, "The lips of my assailants and their whispering are against me all day long."

"My mother said she didn't know anyone by that name. She told my mother it was the lady that speaks English from Liberia, the refugee lady by the name of Martha."

When she heard Bee narrating the story as it was, this wicked lady started crying. The justice of the peace ordered for to immediately be put in jail.

I cried out for her instead. I began to beg on her behalf. "Mr. Justice of Peace, please! I don't want anybody to be put in jail in a strange country." As it is written in God's Word, "It is the glory of God to conceal a matter, but the glory of kings is to search out a matter." The authority handled the matter well, and I was pleased.

I responded to this death threat against me. "We are all Liberians. We have sought refuge in this country. All I want you to do is prevent her from harming me and my family." The court respected my wishes, and let this lady free from any legal charges. The power of forgiveness is a big relief in a person's life. Here's a hint: be sure your sin will find you out. "For there is nothing hidden that will not be disclosed, and nothing concealed that will not be known or brought out into the open," says the Lord. Never pay evil for evil.

A few months after this entire drama, my family and I left and traveled to Ghana. We later heard that after we had gone, so many things happened to the witch lady. One night during a heavy rainstorm, her house collapsed on her. Her brother and two of her children died. She herself had gotten too sick to live with anyone and ended up back in Liberia. From there I don't know what became or happened to her but this I do know: she was forgiven!

Brothers and sisters, whenever you hold fast to Christ, he will see you through! If you keep on keeping on, your strength he will renew! Give your all to him because he took us from disgrace to give us grace. He covers our shame with his blood and lets us shine through his light!

When you ask God to reveal hidden things to you, he will—these are his promises in his Word:

> Ask, and it will be given to you seek, and you will find; knock, and it will be opened to you. (Matthew 7:7)
>
> And whatever you ask in prayer, you will receive, if you have faith." (Matthew 21:22)
>
> Therefore I tell you, whatever you ask in prayer, believe that you have received it, and it will be yours. (Mark 11:24)
>
> Whatever you ask in my name, this I will do, that the Father may be glorified in the Son. If you ask me anything in my name, I will do it. (John 14:13–14)

No matter what it is, ask God.

CHAPTER FIVE

The Path of Life

I HAVE LIVED so many amazing and graceful testimonies in my life time that I can share with you! Do you really have time to listen to them all? They are countless. Let me share some with you. What you see and hear is the power of the loving and living God working in a living vessel.

Life in Danana

Working on Unicef Farm in Danana 1992.

A very productive woman, she used her hands to bring
life back into her home, even as a refugee.

Mom Refugee days in Danana

MARTHA ZEAH GARKPI

Refugee days in Danana

Life in Danana

MARTHA'S STORY

Mom days in Danana making early morning breakfast

While in Danana in 1992, there came a time the citizens of Côte d'Ivoire were counting the number of Liberians who were in Danana. They put a sign on each door of the Liberians. One afternoon, when we came from the refuge farm, we found a paper on our door (which I still have to this day). Before they started counting people, we heard that some Liberian men were helping the Ivoirian forces. The government was trying to send all Liberians back to their home or beat them to stop such behavior. When we came from the farm and saw the number on our door, we were a bit frightened. All we could think about was the possibility of our family being beaten. Our fear stayed with us into the night. I told my children, "Let's not sleep in here tonight. Let's go over to the landlord's house for the night." When we got there, our landlord told us not to be afraid of anything because we had not done anything wrong. If so, he would've known about it. He instructed us to go back home. Nothing happened that night.

Every morning, the girls would get up to bake bread to sell. One morning, as Zamgbah was in the process of baking the bread, she opened the door. It was 4:00 a.m, and she saw these three men coming toward her with military boots on. When she heard the sound of their boots, she ran into the house and closed the door. The men came and began to kick at the door. The news we had been hearing about the government hunting down people made us afraid, remembering the paper being left at the door the day before, and now this? We were mortified! We all began to scream in different voices at the same time. We all were pushing back on the door as the men were trying to kick the door down. I screamed so loud that I almost passed out. At last, one of the men yelled back at us. "Years back, our family used to live in this house, and we are coming from training. We were coming to see them. Sorry for the disturbance." That did not go down well. However, they left, and there was a little rest for the moment.

Later that morning, Zamgbah and I went to the market to purchase some food. After the purchase, I went home, and ZT went to pick up the children from school. From what she told me, she encountered the same army men from the earlier that morning. She thought they were looking for her. Ironically, when I arrived at the house, I saw three men dressed in military clothes walking toward my house. Right then was when I knew those men were up to something. I was so frightened I could feel that my heart was racing. My body froze within the chair I was sitting in. I could not even move nor speak as the men drew closer.

The first thing they asked was, "Mom, what happened?" It took time for me to even answer.

One of them said to me, "Mom, we are your sons. Don't be afraid. We are the ones who were here last night, looking for our family."

When he got through talking, I came to my senses and told them, "You boys have frightened us so badly. I almost died! You all should know that we are from a war-torn country, and with the fear of all we went through, seeing an army is the last thing we want to see. The fear of death comes with them. We are just trying to overcome our fear, so please don't walk up to any Liberian in that manner."

They apologized and left. It was not long until Zamgbah came in with her own story of those same men. What made this really funny was that when we all got together that night and began to reflect on the events of the day, we all went down laughing. I am the mother, and I should be a lot braver. When you picture all of us playing the characters, it is a very funny thing to see.

In 1992, while sleeping one night, something fell to the feet of my girls' bed and touched Judy's feet. She jumped up and began to cry in her deep voice, "Ma, *Ma, Mama*!" We all jumped up from our sleep, and ZT and her husband Larry heard the noise and took a machete (or cutlass) and began to swing it under the bed. We could not risk a thief being there to burglarize us while we slept, to sneak away in the night. He did that for some time, and no one cried out or came out. By now everything that we had stored under the bed was damaged from the machete. I told him to stop so we can check the door and the window. What was crazy was as this was going on, we were calling out for help. We could not speak French, and the people could not understand English. We were screaming "Thief!" when we should've been screaming *"Voleur!"* No task is too large or too difficult for him (Jeremiah 32:17, 27).

Danana: The Life Lessons

This story took place in Danana, Nyinle, with our landlord's sister. This lady had been blind for many, many years. In 1993, her husband asked if he could wash her clothes for Sunday, and she answered, "No!"

"Why?" he replied.

"I can't find one of my slippers." She expressed, "God hasn't been good to me, so I am not going to church anymore."

With all of that, her husband still went ahead and did the washing. The clothes did not get dry that day. The sun was shining, but her clothes remained wet.

When it was time to go to church, her husband left her home. While sitting at home alone, a bug flew over her head and hit her face. Her eyes opened, and then she saw a man walking toward her. In this man's hand was the slipper that she had been looking for. He gave it to her. Sitting with no emotion, she then asked about his name.

He said, "My name is Mai-ka-siea, Bia-ka-yeah." In Gio, it means "I have done well. You have spoiled it." When he finished speaking, he started moving on.

All of a sudden, another bug came and hit her face again, and she went back to being blind. At this moment, she went to the church. She was crying, telling everyone that she saw Jesus and he brought her slipper back to her. "I was not appreciative. I was asking him questions, and now I cannot see again."

This is a true story. When God brings us in a new state of life, let's learn to be people who express our emotion to and about God when they are excited. All she could have done was shout "Hallelujah!" and run to the church praising God. Now she is talking about what he has done, even though God has reversed her miracle. *God is everywhere and no one can escape him (Ps. 139:7–12).*

Be careful with God, as he is ever-present. Your blessing is just in reach. It is up to you to receive it.

> Where can I go from Your Spirit? Where can I flee from your presence? If I go up to the heavens, you are there; if I make my bed in the depths, you are there. If I rise on the wings of the dawn, if I settle on the far side of the sea, even there your hand will guide me, Your right hand will hold me fast. If I say, "Surely the darkness will hide me and the light become night around me," even the darkness will not be dark to You; the night will shine like the day, for darkness is as light to You. (Psalm 139:7–12)

New Life in a New Place: Accra, Ghana

Refugee days in Ghana

Grandma mamie in Ghana

MARTHA ZEAH GARKPI

My days in Ghana

My days my girls and I Ghana

MARTHA'S STORY

There are many things to consider when stepping out into something new. We move out in faith when we know we want a new life. My family did just that and continued to pursue their education while we were in Ghana. The furthering of my children's education was a big joy to me and the Horaces.

Relocating can be stressful for anybody, even if the move is a positive change for you. Leaving the familiar embrace of your loved ones for somewhere unknown can be very hard, and there can be some difficulties adjusting to the new changes. One may ask themselves: How will you find your way around? How will you make new friends? How will you keep up with your old friends you've made in your previous location? Above all that, you may have some thoughts: Did I really make the right decision? What if I had gotten ahead of myself? Did I hear from the Lord?

We waited until the Lord told us to move, because he always knows best. The foundation was planned very carefully and, as a result, stood very strong.

How I missed the large farms we made and were a part of in Danana. The somewhat country living was a beautiful experience—free flowing as each day goes by for us.

We heard from people coming back and forth from Ghana about the living conditions. Based on those assessments, we took the leap of faith. My daughter Kosiapoe and her husband had encouraged us to move to Ghana so that we could have another life. The girls could go to school there, being it was not possible in Côte d'Ivoire. They made it possible, with the help of the Lord, for us to move to Accra, Ghana, on September 9, 1993. They placed cash—US $1,000—in the express mail to one of my nieces, Elfreda Johnson, who was living in Ghana at the time. That money was misplaced for over six months! With lot of prayer, God allowed us to track it down. The envelope was all beat up, but God had his eyes on it. Big thanks to Kosiapoe and her husband for their continuous love to me and all the family. That initial $1,000 made our move very smooth. We made ourselves very happy and comfortable and adapted to the culture and the good lifestyles of the indigenous.

Our first move was finding a spiritual covering. We found a beautiful church that we could be a part of. We were taught the Word and given great love. Lighthouse Baptist Church was our home church, which we attended and became members of. The brethren of the church were there for us spiritually and naturally every day. They opened their arms and received us in every way in the church.

We found a house we could rent in Nungua, Accra, in Rock City. We stayed there for five months, until we decided to leave. There were many religious biases, and for this reason we had to relocate. Oh, the things we go through for our faith! Despite all adversity, I stand by my beliefs.

We found a house to rent in March 1994, but the stay was short-lived. We lived there less than a year, and again, differences got the best of us. We had to find somewhere else to go. When you encounter different people from different areas and walks of life, there are going to be issues that you cannot smooth over. This is when the love of God comes in. No matter where you come from and what you've done, God's love remains the same. No man can change your destiny!

We then moved to an area called Nautical College, at one Mr. Ray's house, where we dwelled for about two years.

We moved to Nuagua, Coco Beach, after some time because Kosiapoe and her husband were bringing their babies to us from USA. The place we had was not spacious enough for all of us, so we moved in June of 1996. We lived there for about two years.

Coming through the war was through the power of God. All praises are due to him, for faith in Christ is the fullness we need in securing our lives. One good thing that ever came from the war was that people were closer to God than ever before. Many of the young people went to Bible College and became great preachers.

Right in my house at Coco Beach, we started a Bible study class. Later on it became a big group. We started out with one pastor, Edwin Gbor, and later on, Dahn Demey and Augusta King were added as pastors too. They came to us from the Bible College as they worked on their churches. The church received others from the Bible College too: Michael Thomas, Joe Thomas, and Papou Thomas.

The church grew, and our first leader went home to Liberia. Pastor Dahn Demey would then become one of our lead pastors. When they left to go home to build their churches, we missed him and Pastor Gbor. We knew they had to do the work God had called them to. These two churches are still functioning today—Pastor Gbor is in Ganta, Nimba County, and Pastor Demey is in Monrovia, Liberia. This is due to their being faithful and willing to be used by God.

Being in the group with other believers strengthened us in so many special ways. We had a special care one for the other, which was a blessing for each one of us. There were not only Liberians in the spiritual group. People of many different nationalities were among us. We all achieved a lot from the group. When one was down, the whole group came in to meet their need. We cheered each other up too! Being their spiritual mother was a big responsibility for me.

The name of our group was the Refuge Fellowship. There is nothing greater than getting love from your Christian brothers and sisters. Proverbs 17:17 says, "A friend loveth at all times." We had the love of God and each other. We had a real big church in Danana, Côte d'Ivoire, with the same name as the church in Liberia: Refuge Fellowship.

While in Ghana, we had a family member, Elfreda, and some friends that were nice to us until they left for the United Kingdom. I thank God for them in many ways.

Our stay in Ghana was a great blessing to many Liberian families again. Just like how I lived in Liberia, this was the same lifestyle. God began to change our life circumstances by putting Ghanaian friends in our path, along with church families. I cared for family members' children—the old and young passed through with joy. I accommodated everyone with comfort. It is not your location in life—it is you that can change your environment to continue to affect people's lives.

We were involved in all activities of the church. The children sang in the choir, and I headed the Women's Department. Dayanah headed the Youth Department as well as worked with the young people from Liberia. She had formed a singing group called the Redeemed Voices of the Lighthouse Baptist Church. They sang from church to church as they were called upon to.

The members of the group were

Michel Thomas, President	Dayanah B. Soeh, lead singer
Edwin Gbor	Degusia P. Soeh
Mercy Krua	Maybel Kpah
Joan Krua	Baby Boy Kpahn
Joseph Huge	Sam Kpahn
Brother Maxwell	Kayitomou Kleh
Amanda Sorrow	

Sis Rebecca Mayu and I were the mothers of the group.

Here are the names of our pastors, leaders, and some members of LightHouse Baptist Church:

Pastor James Kori	Mr. Charles Jetuh
Mr. Victor Anndor	Mr. Adu Peprah
Mr. Daniel Baisie	Mrs. Joanna Kori
Sister Stella Kodie	Brother Enoch Kewin Fosu
Brother Persper Piere	Brother Joseph T. Gurash
and many more	

I also had some spiritual children: James M. and Tina Ndego. The family was very nice to us. They had four children: Mboard Ndego, Jameel M., Latifa, and Frank.

While at Nautical, a strange thing happened to Brother Anndor, one of the Sunday School teachers, on a Tuesday while at work. His boss asked him to go food shopping. He said while sitting down at his desk, he saw me before him looking at him. First, he said he called my name, and he didn't see me again. He then wondered if something bad had happened to us.

He said he left to go to the market with a lady from the office to buy the foodstuff. After shopping, he went back to where he left off in his head. He then again saw me standing before him. So he felt heavier and sorrowful in his heart. He told the lady to take the food to the office.

He came to check on his spiritual mother and her children. He brought with him some food and other things we would need. When he arrived, he found me sick. We had no money and no food either at my house. He said he knew there was something wrong because he was troubled in his spirit that day and the night before.

Then he said that he saw me in a vision. From that day he had that vision, he sent food to us every week. That's how much God loves me and my family. He said in Philippians 4:19 that he will supply all our needs, according to his riches and glory through Christ Jesus.

There came a time when there were many people at the house. Family and friends who had no food were welcome to come break bread with us. Even though it seemed that there wouldn't be enough food, God always provided to where everyone had enough to be full.

One day, we went to church, and I gave my praise report. I let them know that God still works miracles. He did perform a miracle in our kitchen and in our pots each time we cooked; there was always enough.

MARTHA ZEAH GARKPI

This was where I really had to have faith in God and his miracle-working power. The closer we get to God, the hungrier we must get for the Word, the Bible.

Matthew 5:6 says, "Blessed are they which do hunger and thirst after righteousness, for they shall be filled."

Psalm 107:9 says, "For he satisfieth the longing soul and filleth the hungry soul with goodness."

Psalm 55:22 says, "Cast thy burden upon the LORD, and he shall sustain thee: he shall never suffer the righteous to be moved." Without God, we can do nothing.

Our Stay in Liberia

Calvary Baptist School days Liberia

December 27, 1998, was the day when the Liberians were allowed back home by order of the UN. When we arrived back home, we found that things weren't as good as we were led to believe. But nonetheless, home is home.

We were asked to leave our residence in Nungua, Coco Beach, for repatriation. Leaving one's comfort zone is not an easy thing. You get a strange feeling when you leave a place, like you will not only miss the people you love, but you will miss the person you were at that time and place. No matter how you comfort yourself, the homesickness will return. Sometimes, it never happens. My church families were phenomenal to us in all of our travels, though some experiences were challenging, like the Danana life-and-death experiences. Presently, I have not gone back to all those African countries my children and I took refuge in. I look forward to going back one day.

After many days, we arrived in Liberia, singing "Sweet Land of Liberty."

> All hail, Liberia, hail! (repeat)
> This glorious land of liberty shall long be ours.
> Though new her name, Green be her fame,
>
> And mighty be her powers, (repeat)
> In joy and gladness With our hearts united,
> We'll shout the freedom of a race benighted,
> Long live Liberia, happy land! A home of glorious liberty,
>
> By God's command! (Repeat last two sentences)

My homes were all full of family members who came back after the war ended. We worked out the transition and were all happy to see each other. My children and I moved into the five-bedroom house in the front and left the other family members in the original house.

Some neighbors were happy to see us, and others weren't. The guilt they felt from the looting they had done to our homes was probably the reason. Some of them never wanted us to return. Nevertheless, we were home at last. There is no place like home. According to some African cultures, when you travel from afar, you have to bring gifts home. I carried on tradition, bringing all sorts of things to share. Oh, how that broke a lot of ice, and everything began to flow.

It was sad to know that most of the women in our neighborhood had lost their husbands at the Lutheran church massacre back in 1990. We all comforted each other, and luckily enough, some of us were members of the same church.

We started on the right foot by serving our God as we had always done. We were grateful that God brought us back home safely. We got in and fellowshipped with our church, Beawo Baptist, which was our home church in Sinkor, as we did before the war. The reunion was great! Many tears and lots of joy flowed from each person. Overall, we all were happy to see each other. All of my children had grown now after those many years. Everyone was out of high school and had a trade certificate prior to our return, thanks to the Horaces.

My third daughter, Dayanah, got married to Mr. Michael Thomas while in Liberia. He had also lived in Ghana.

My eldest daughter, Kosiapoe, spent her youth in this church where she taught children Sunday school class until she was married to Bishop Horace on April 29, 1989. This was a few months before the Liberian Civil War in 1990.

Some of my family came from Nimba to unite with us after many years of being away. One of these people was one of my oldest cousins, Goulou Wehyee, who was a mother figure to me. Beautiful reunions! There was also a surprise visit from my sister Darcy.

There is an end to everything in life, which is a known fact. The Bible specifically testifies of that in Ecclesiastes 3:1–8 NIV:

> There is a time for everything, and a season for every activity under the heavens: a time to be born and a time to die, a time to plant and a time to uproot, a time to kill and a time to heal, a time to tear down and a time

to build, a time to weep and a time to laugh, a time to mourn and a time to dance, a time to scatter stones and a time to gather them, a time to embrace and a time to refrain from embracing, a time to search and a time to give up, a time to keep and a time to throw away, a time to tear and a time to mend, a time to be silent and a time to speak, a time to love and a time to hate, a time for war and a time for peace.

Bearing in mind that we are here for such a short time frame, we have to be careful as to how much we have God in the equation of everything we do. July 19, 1999, Darcy, my ex-husband's girlfriend, showed up at my Fourteenth Street residence. This time, it was different. She came down to my feet in repentance, apologizing for taking my husband, the father of my children, away from us. What else could be said? The years of damage have been done. Lives have been ruined! I contemplated on all the things I have wanted to say to her when the time came. Then, I asked her this question: "Where is he now?" There was no answer!

I said, "It's my understanding that he is still the same?" I reminded her that in life, one cannot remain young always. Age has a way of showing up, and the body has a way of saying you won't have many good times much longer because old age must come. None of us had to go through this. It was out of kindness that I asked my husband to give her a ride home. Instead, it turned out negatively for me. Remember, you have control over what you allow to get to you, and what you decide to fight over in a relationship. Having said all of that, I knew in my heart I had no alternative but to forgive her. A point of reconciliation is one of the strongest weapons you can wield. All consequences were between her and her God. This was in the presence of my daughter Mercy and her husband. They had come to visit us from the USA. My foster parents, the late Reverend John K. Demey and his wife Ma Mary Demey, Lucy and a family member of hers, and others were present as well. The family values of love and forgiveness were exhibited that day.

MARTHA ZEAH GARKPI

After two months of the Horaces being with us in Liberia, my daughter Kosiapoe told me, "Sister, about this time next year, we will be in the USA together."

I believed her and said, "Yes, there is a time for everything."

Secondly, I missed my babies Emmanuel and Emmuel. I really wanted to see my grandchildren because I haven't seen them since they lived with us in Ghana for one year. We could not wait until it was time for my trip. All praises are to God. The foundation of a strong family is standing on the Word of God and his promises.

CHAPTER SIX

God Is . . .

My Life's Purpose

My day at Alpha Child Development Center

Serving the King at Living Word Food Pantry

I PRAY FOR A fruitful, purposeful, and useful living. Despite it all, the good and the bad, I give the Lord praise. We need to learn from Jesus. He lived a most satisfying life—pleasing to God and fulfilling all that the Father expected from him. I wonder why we don't want to be more like him.

Jesus never had to ask the question, "Why am I here on Earth?" It was clearly prophesied even before he was born. His parents needed not to have to think of a name for him, like all parents do. His name was given even before he was born. His name represented his entire life and purpose: he was born to save. Sometimes I laugh at my name Martha. I served all my life but always made time to spend with God.

Born in Bethlehem. Micah 5:2 says, "But you, Bethlehem Ephrathah, though you are small among the clans of Judah, out of you will come for me one who will be ruler over Israel, whose origins are from of old, from ancient times." The story of Jesus's birth in Bethlehem is told in the New Testament books of Matthew, Luke, and John. Think about your location of birth. I was born at the creek.

Born of a virgin. Isaiah 7:14 says, "Therefore the Lord himself will give you a sign: The virgin will be with child and will give birth to a son, and will call him Immanuel." The New Testament book of Matthew repeats this prophecy in a passage detailing Joseph's encounter with an angel of the Lord, who tells Joseph that Mary's child was conceived by the Holy Spirit and will save his people from their sins. Who was or is your mother? My mother was a woman who went on an adventure, very pregnant.

Born among sorrow. Jesus's birth fulfills a prophecy in Jeremiah 31:15: "A voice is heard in Ramah, mourning and great weeping. Rachel weeping for her children and refusing to be comforted, because her children are no more." This prophecy is repeated in the book of Matthew, which says that King Herod sought to kill Jesus. "When Herod realized that he had been outwitted by the Magi, he was furious, and he gave orders to kill all the boys in Bethlehem and its vicinity who were two years old and under, in accordance with the time he had learned from the Magi. Then what was said through the prophet Jeremiah was fulfilled" (Matthew 2:16). What surrounded your birth? I was born during a time of famine. My parents worked hard for us to survive.

He lived only for thirty-three years and completed what he was born to do. From his encounter with this Samaritan woman, Jesus showed us three guiding principles of life: (1) he lived his life knowing his purpose, (2) he had the right priorities, and (3) he was driven by a passion to fulfill God's will.

I pray that everyone lives their life knowing their true purpose.

Jesus and his disciples were on their way to Judea from the north (Galilee). If they had taken the normal route, they would not have passed Samaria. In fact, there are at least three different routes from Galilee to Judea, yet Jesus made a stop at this place, Samaria.

December 15, 1949, my parents came to this little town called Zia to give birth to me on the banks of a creek called Zuogbalua. I was told that the people in that village would only go fishing once every year at that creek. My mother, at this particular time, gave birth to me on that one special fishing trip. It was in God's plan that they were not from Zia, just as mentioned about Jesus coming to Samaria.

Why? He knows his purpose: to bring the message of God's love to this Samaritan woman. He has come to meet the woman at the well and give her the message of new life that he can offer, "living water." And did he succeed? Yes—in fact, very well. Looking back at my own life, the above is reflected today. My life is nothing short of a miracle. I was born in a cold bush on a green leaf and was brought to town in a fishing net. Look at this path! The place I was born was the very same place I died at the age of three. This time, my mother came by herself to back to Zia. I am a miracle child! This is my testimony. What God has done for me, I cannot tell it all. This is the amazing story of my life. In 1952, Evangelist Mealekpeh Garkpi came to our village to preach the Gospel. He went home with a child for his wife, which was not expected of him. Due to the purpose that God had for my life, he allowed this transition. God knows everything. "He determines the course of world events; He removes kings and sets others on the throne. He gives wisdom to the wise and knowledge to the scholars" (Daniel 2:21).

Who God Is

God is faithful.

> Know therefore that the Lord your God is God, the faithful God who keeps covenant and steadfast love with those who love him and keep his commandments, to a thousand generations. (Deuteronomy 7:9 ESV)

Your steadfast love, O Lord, extends to the heavens, your faithfulness to the clouds. (Psalm 36:5 ESV)

The steadfast love of the Lord never ceases his mercies never come to an end; they are new every morning; great is your faithfulness. (Lamentations 3:22–23 ESV)

Let us hold fast the confession of our hope without wavering, for he who promised is faithful. (Hebrews 10:23 ESV)

God is not man, that he should lie, or a son of man, that he should change his mind. Has he said, and will he not do it? Or has he spoken, and will he not fulfill it? (Numbers 23:19 ESV)

God's love is forever proven.

The Lord your God is in your midst, a mighty one who will save;

he will rejoice over you with gladness; he will quiet you by his love;

he will exult over you with loud singing. (Zephaniah 3:17 ESV)

But you, O Lord, are a God merciful and gracious,

slow to anger and abounding in steadfast love and faithfulness. (Psalm 86:15 ESV)

But I say to you, Love your enemies and pray for those who persecute you, so that you may be sons of your Father who is in heaven. For he makes his sun rise on the evil and on the good, and sends rain on the just and on the unjust. (Matthew 5:44–45 ESV)

I love those who love me, and those who seek me diligently find me. (Proverbs 8:17 ESV)

A new commandment I give to you, that you love one another: just as I have loved you, you also are to love one another. By this all people will know that you are my disciples, if you have love for one another. (John 13:34–35 ESV)

God is just at all times.

God is just: He will pay back trouble to those who trouble you. (2 Thessalonians 1:6 KJV)

That be far from thee to do after this manner, to slay the righteous with the wicked: and that the righteous should be as the wicked, that be far from thee: Shall not the Judge of all the earth do right? (Genesis 18:25 KJV)

He is the Rock, his works are perfect, and all his ways are just. A faithful God who does no wrong, upright and just is he. (Deuteronomy 32:5 KJV)

He hath shewed thee, O man, what is good; and what doth the Lord require of thee, but to do justly, and to love mercy, and to walk humbly with thy God? (Micah 6:8 KJV)

I the Lord search the heart, I try the reins, even to give every man according to his ways, and according to the fruit of his doings. (Jeremiah 17:10 KJV)

God's sovereignty is a guide to me.

Our God is in the heavens; he does all that he please.
(Psalm 115:3 ESV)

And we know that for those who love God all things
work together for good, for those who are called
according to his purpose. For those whom he foreknew
he also predestined to be conformed to the image of
his Son, in order that he might be the firstborn among
many brothers. And those whom he predestined
he also called, and those whom he called he also
justified, and those whom he justified he also glorified.
(Romans 8:28–30 ESV)

The plans of the heart belong to man, but the answer
of the tongue is from the Lord. All the ways of a man
are pure in his own eyes, but the Lord weighs the spirit.
Commit your work to the Lord, and your plans will
be established. The Lord has made everything for
its purpose, even the wicked for the day of trouble.
(Proverbs 16:1–4 ESV)

You will say to me then, "Why does he still find fault?
For who can resist his will?" (Romans 9:19 ESV)

While the man of God was preaching, I fell asleep. This was not a
regular nap. I was dead on my mother's lap at three years old. I was not
breathing and was pronounced dead. The evangelist was told to bring
me back to life or else; he was threatened.

According to him, he then stretched over me and prayed. "O God of
Abraham, Isaac and Jacob, you are the God of yesterday, today, and
forever. Bring this girl to life so your name will be praised, so the people
in this village can believe in you." God answered his prayers after many
hours. When we think about Jesus and all he has done for us, our souls
cry out *Hallelujah*!"

　　　MARTHA ZEAH GARKPI

My Daily Walk with God

Every day is a day with the Lord! Things I experienced in life were very difficult, and I know that without Christ, I would have long gone from this world. Satan, the enemy of our soul, means us no good. I learned Christ in all of my travels, but more than that, I learned me! Who I am or ever hope to be is because of God!

I started knowing myself. I am afraid sometimes to say things out loud to God. The reason being, whenever someone is trying to do harm to me and I cry out his name, he avenges on my behalf. The Lord has been so good to me all of my life. I can't complain.

He healed the sick, the brokenhearted, the lost. He fed those who were hungry, raised the dead. He met the needs of the world, and he gave his life as a living sacrifice! We are his, and he is ours.

I am a miracle child. I have found him to be real through all of my life experiences. On the one hand, we choose to do well, but then we do something else. That's not good! If you do me well, God blesses you well! God has been performing miracles in my life since I was born!

How did this happen? God's plan for our lives cannot be destroyed by the devil. God knew this was the path. He had to give a child to this evangelist and his wife. Whatever it takes, God will provide and make many provisions in his infinite power.

The Power of Prayer

Mother's Dream (Mercy Educational Foundation) Liberia

MARTHA ZEAH GARKPI

Mother's Dream (Mercy Educational Foundation) Liberia

The final stage of her educational dream was building a school in Liberia.

When God is on your side, you need not worry. God's word is a lamp to our feet, a light to our path. Seeing myself today as I am, I know it is only through faith. Faith is powerful and wonderful, and it can change one's life circumstance. I never look down on myself. When I look at a situation in my life, I continue to speak the Word of God over the circumstances; and by faith, my situation changes. Faith is having the ability to see what is real and begin to speak newness into existence. It is the ability to look at what is and what is not and cause it to be what you desire it to be. God elevated me from a nowhere state to a somewhere state. To God be the glory!

"And we know that in all things God works for the good of those who love him, who have been called according to his purpose. For those God foreknew he also predestined to be conformed to the image of his Son, that he might be the firstborn among many brothers and sisters" (Romans 8:28–29 NIV). This is my testimony for this purpose. He changed my life!

Like I said, God brought me into this world for a reason. If you have reached this far in my book, you can see the miracles he did to keep me alive. We aren't going anywhere until he says so. I have and still do pray God's will be done in my life.

Philippians 4:19 says, "And my God will supply all your needs according to his riches in glory in Christ Jesus." In Matthew 6:26, we find, "Look at the birds of the air, that they do not sow, nor reap nor gather into barns, and yet your heavenly Father feeds them. Are you not worth much more than they?" Psalm 81:10 adds, "I, the LORD, am your God, Who brought you up from the land of Egypt; Open your mouth wide and I will fill it."

We can hide from man, but not God. See how God brought the driver right to us? God will not have his children treated any kind of way, especially when man feels they can outdo God. When God says yes, no man can say no! God always fights for me, and he will fight for you too! As the Word says, "God's Word is our defense."

> And Moses said to the people, "Do not be afraid. Stand still, and see the salvation of the LORD, which he will accomplish for you today. For the Egyptians whom you see today, you shall see again no more forever. The LORD will fight for you, and you shall hold your peace." (Exodus 14:13–14)

> Many are the afflictions of the righteous, but the LORD delivers him out of them all. (Psalm 34:19)

> A thousand may fall at your side, and ten thousand at your right hand; but it shall not come near you. (Psalm 91:7)

> The LORD is good, a stronghold in the day of trouble; and he knows those who trust in him." (Nahum 1:7)

> We are hard-pressed on every side, yet not crushed; we are perplexed, but not in despair; persecuted, but not forsaken; struck down, but not destroyed. (2 Corinthians 4:8–9)

> Naaman's servants went to him and said, "My father, if the prophet had told you to do some great thing, would you not have done it? How much more, then, when he tells you, 'Wash and be cleansed'!" So he went down and dipped himself in the Jordan seven times, as the man of God had told him, and his flesh was restored and became clean like that of a young boy. Then Naaman and all his attendants went back to the man of God. He stood before him and said, "Now I know that there is no God in all the world except in

Israel. So please accept a gift from your servant." (2 Kings 5:13–15)

Trust in the Lord with all your heart, and do not lean on your own understanding. (Proverbs 3:5)

Delight yourself in the Lord, and he will give you the desires of your heart. Commit your way to the Lord; trust in him, and he will act. He will bring forth your righteousness as the light, and your justice as the noonday. (Psalm 37:4–6)

And we know that for those who love God all things work together for good, for those who are called according to his purpose. (Romans 8:28)

In all your ways acknowledge him, and he will make straight your paths.

I stood on these verses for Life and Light daily. (Proverbs 3:6)

The Power of God's Words

Mom days @ LWCCI with her Sr. Pastor Bishop Bedell Horace

Life @ Living Word

In all the changes I found myself in life, God brought me out of them with his outstretched hands. Whether my calls to him were at night, day, or noon, he shows up when I pray. He knows when Martha called. Whether it was long or short, I felt his presence and I saw an answer. There have been many divine encounters you've read about in this book. None of them were of my might or my power. It was all by his spirit. The night of the Lutheran church massacre, while lying there in the front foyer of the Methodist church, I was very fearful of what would happen if any of the death squad knew that people were in an open edifice. No one would have survived to tell the story. There were no open windows, only two doors, which were locked. All we could do was lie there. I heard the Lord say, "Be still and know that I am God."

Something very strange happened that night. We had a half bag of rice with us that we managed to have located in our home when we took Love for treatment after we left the Lutheran church. The night of the killing at the Lutheran church, we were lying so still, there was no reason to not have heard the bag of rice disappear. The morning we were running for our lives, I told Kosiapoe to take the rice, put it in the baby tub, and carry it on her head.

She said, "I can't find the rice."

"What!" The rice could not be found. I said, "Lord, if the death angel took it, thank you for sparing me. Now we have no food, but, God, you will provide for us and as you have been doing."

Ephesians 6:18 (ESV) says "Praying at all times the Spirit, with all prayer and supplication. To that end, keep alert with all perseverance, making supplication for all the saints."

The power of prayer is not the result of the one praying. Rather, the power rests in God's ability. The First Book of John 5:14–15 tells us, "This is the confidence we have in approaching God: that if we ask anything according to his will, he hears us. And if we know that he

MARTHA ZEAH GARKPI

hears us—whatever we ask—we know that we have what we asked of him." No matter the person praying, the passion behind the prayer, or the purpose of the prayer, God answers prayers that are in agreement with his will. His answers are not always yes but are always in our best interest. When our desires line up with his will, we will come to understand that in time. When we pray passionately and purposefully, according to God's will, God responds powerfully!

We have many accounts in the Bible that describes the power of prayer in different situations. It helps us to believe that if God did it before, he can do it again. The power of prayer has overcome our enemies (Psalm 6:9–10), conquered deaths (2 Kings 44:3–36, James 5:14–15), and healed and defeated demons (Mark 9:29). When we pray, God opens our eyes, changes hearts, heals wounds, and grants wisdom in whatever our need may be. The power of prayer should never be underestimated because it draws on the glory and might of the infinitely powerful God. Daniel prayed when he was in the lion's den, and God answered and delivered him. Elijah brought the widow's son back to life. On the day that the Lord gave the Amorites over to Israel, Joshua said to the Lord in the presence of Israel, "Sun, stand still over Gideon, and you, moon, over the Valley of Aijalon." And God did. God does what he wants to do and when he wants. He does as he pleases with the powers of heaven and the peoples of the earth. No one can hold back God's hands or say to him, "What have you done, and why have you done it?" Abraham prayed to God, and God healed Abimelech and his wife and his maids so that they bore children.

> The children of Israel prayed, and the Lord said, "I have surely seen the affliction of my people who are in Egypt, and have given heed to their cry because of their taskmasters, for I am aware of their sufferings. So I have come down to deliver them from the power of the Egyptians, and to bring them up from that land to a good and spacious land, to a land flowing with milk and honey, to the place of the Canaanite and the

Hittite and the Amorite and the Perizzite and the Hivite and the Jebusite. Now, behold, the cry of the sons of Israel has come to me; furthermore, I have seen the oppression with which the Egyptians are oppressing them." (Exodus 3:7–8)

When Moses called on the Lord, then the Lord said to Moses, "Why are you crying out to Me? Tell the sons of Israel to go forward. As for you, lift up your staff and stretch out your hand over the sea and divide it, and the sons of Israel shall go through the midst of the sea on dry land." (Exodus 14:15–16)

Hannah prayed to the Lord in great distress and wept bitterly. She made a vow and said, "O LORD of hosts, if you will indeed look on the affliction of Your maidservant and remember me, and not forget Your maidservant, but will give Your maidservant a son, then I will give him to the LORD all the days of his life, and a razor shall never come on his head." Now it came about, as she continued praying before the Lord, that Eli was watching her mouth. (I Samuel 1:11)

Elijah prayed for his servant and said, "O LORD, I pray, open his eyes that he may see." And the Lord opened the servant's eyes, and he saw; and behold, the mountain was full of horses and chariots of fire all around Elisha. When they came down to him, Elisha prayed to the Lord and said, "Strike this people with blindness, I pray." So he struck them with blindness according to the word of Elisha. Then Elisha said to them, "This is not the way, nor is this city; follow me and I will bring you to the man whom you seek." And he brought them to Samaria. (II Kings 6:17–18)

MARTHA ZEAH GARKPI

Even in Zacharias's old age, an angel and said to him, "Do not be afraid, Zacharias, for your petition has been heard, and your wife Elizabeth will bear you a son, and you will give him the name John." (Luke 1:13)

Even the leper came to him and bowed down before him, and said, "Lord, if you are willing, You can make me clean." Jesus stretched out his hand and touched him, saying, "I am willing; be cleansed." And immediately his leprosy was cleansed. (Luke 5:12–13)

God has not changed. He is the same yesterday, today, and forever. No matter your petitions, bring them to God. Satan can't have your marriage, your children, your finances—you name it, he can't! God is able to complete everything he has begun in you. Fear not!

Laughter Is the Best Medicine

Mom at church

Pa and Ma Krua were missionaries to Zia, and they were very understanding people. Whenever Pa would say things that were not okay to her, all she did was look at him and call his name. She would politely look and say "Kolay." He would quickly change the topic! Other times, she would just say, "Give me a drink of water." Right away he knew what that meant. What an amazing way to build your relationship on good understanding. Pa Krua, you will remember Ma Esther in many ways for that. One thing most Gio women could not do is cook rice. They just put rice in the pot and cook. But not Ma Esther—she knew the mathematics of rice cooking. She knew how many cups of rice to take out that would be enough for the whole family. Even when someone else came over to visit, she had just enough. She did this from day 1 till the time she became sick and came to the United States of America. All in all, she was a smart woman, although she never went to school. When she came to America, she learned how to read the Holy Bible in English and even explained it in Gio. The greatness of God!

Pastor and Mrs. Krua went to Zia as evangelists. They even built a school there! That's where Old Man Kpah learned English.

Ma Martha had two children close to each other in age, a boy and a girl. She asked her husband to name the children. He actually named them "Boy "and "Girl." People asked him why? He would say, "Because I love English!"

During devotion one day in Zia, it was said to us, "Tonight, let all the boys and girls stand to their feet!" Old Man Kpah had to pray.

His wife asked him, "Kpah, if God called you today, would you be willing to go?"

Right away, he started another song in English, "Come to Jesus Right Now."

We all laughed along with Martha.

MARTHA ZEAH GARKPI

Bible School Students

In Bible school, we were taught to give 10 percent of everything. Money or fruits from harvest were ideal to be our tithe. Even kids were taught to give. Mr. and Mrs. Freeman Sawhy had ten children. The tenth was to be given to the church. Then the church was fully responsible for the child's upbringing. There was a race between the few women of Mid-Baptist Mission, such as Mrs. Wydorea, Mrs. Demey, Mrs. Kpou, Mrs. Mayu, Mrs. Kwena and Mrs. Krua. Most of these women had more than seven children! Besides their own children, they took care of the children of the community as well. Many lives were touched by them. There were so many others I don't have time to name them all. Thank God for them all!

Fun, Fun Times

You will have to be from Zia or Tappita to really laugh at these jokes. I won't even have to end the joke, and some of my readers will already start laughing.

1. *Borber Bodou.* Speaking English to Reverend Holmes (missing days of school).
2. *Oldman Sawi Kpou.* When he came from the US in the seventies, he said to his wife, Kenyonnoh, "Fix me some salad." He forgot where he was. In the deep villages of Africa, there is no salad! His wife had no idea what salad was.
3. *Moses Wazea.* Teacher I come from WC.
4. *Mr. Druo.* Preaching in English. Topic: Druo was fine.
5. *Old Man Garkpi.* His favorite saying to his wife was "JJY." As a man speaking English, all she assumed was that JJY was an insult. She would start crying. *JJY* was an ethnic word in Bassa.
6. *Gbenda Mellish.* His favorite saying was "Go to bed!" His wife Margaret would say, "Why go to bed?" His answer was for them to grow. "They are not growing. Kay and Carolyn are still the same."

7. Reverend Demey's brother *Glee Peter* and his wife lived in Zoulai. His wife (Rachel) would walk from there to Tappita to come tell on Peter (her husband). He had insulted her. When she got to Tappita to tell of the fight, she had forgotten what had happened.

8. Rev. Demey's brother *Gbon*. He did not like the way white people gave names to his family (Martha and Nancy, Demey Mothers, Vonyee).

9. *Ma Mary Zonua, Ma Sarah Mayu,* and *Ma Esther Vannie* were reading a letter about a sick person needing an airplane to be transported. They looked at the letter upside-down and pretended to read. They were going off of what they heard the person was telling them in Gio, because none of them could read English.

10. *Cousin Emma* would to say to her kids, "Get in the tub." Her sister Margaret said, "Gbenda says, 'Go to bed.' You say, 'Get in the tub.' My ears are hurting from all this English!"

11. *Old Man Gblozou*. He came from up from the interior of Nimba County to go to Monrovia to sing for President Tubman! He's singing with his nose: "[Dee] looks like a crazy, oh! And a come to me like a palm wine, oh" (and the rhythm goes on in African slang).

    a. Driver *Sunkala—Gblozou Wheyee* runs fast like a dog after a deer!

    b. *Sunkala—Gblozou Wheyee*. Grey coat? "You buy like girl before you born like child? Or you born la child before buy la girl or why?" (He is speaking in his nose.) This person is asking a question in broken Liberian English.

    c. *Sunkala—Gblozou Wheyee*. They had an accident on their way to their hometown. (His driver was in the wrong. He had to pay for the damages but had no money.)

    d. *Mr. Wheyee* paid for damages but asked to be paid back with a duck from their farm.

The name of the duck was *Quie-tuah* in Gio, meaning "English name." It could be John, Peter or Mary. When it was time for them to pay back the money with the duck, they ask the man, "What type of name you like, John or Peter?" He told them he did not want to talk about an English name for a duck. They said "When we said *quie-tuah* you did not ask us what kind of *quie-tuah*." That was the end of the matter!

When we came from Ghana, the church gave us a singing clock as a gift. This clock sang every hour on the hour. One day when we went to sleep, in my dream I felt that someone was entering the house. So I sat up in bed, looked straight at the open window. I saw a hand trying to open the window screen. They manage to get into the window. When the clock hand went toward the twelve, the clock began to sing. The person let go of the window, and all I heard was a running sound outside. Right then, I began calling for help, and someone came to our aid. From that day, we always closed the windows and the door very well before going to bed. The funny part about it is that the thief never thought that we had something in our home that could frighten them off. From that day, rumors went around that that house is well armed. All that happened was the divine act of God. He may not come when you want him, but he's right on time!

Coming to America

When it was time for me to come to the USA, nothing could stop the plans of God. We tried so many times in Ghana, but it was not the time that God saw fit. An invitation from my daughter Kosiapoe and her husband to come and spend Christmas with them in December 1999 was a big joy and an answer to my prayers. There was no question about the invitation. I was given my visa immediately.

I encountered an unfortunate incident while at the airport in Ivory Coast, en route to the United States. It was December 24, 1999. The government of President Henri Konan Bedie was deposed in coup d'état led by an army general, Robert Gay. Whenever there is political conflict in the Ivory Coast, the negative treatment of foreigners always heightens.

A spokesman for Mr. Ouattara told Reuters that the former prime minister fled his home as troops arrived. The aide said he did not know where the leader was. A court fight over Mr. Ouattara's eligibility to stand for elections caused massive controversy in the country, but his party was recently invited to participate in government.

The uprising saw heavy fighting break out in and around Abidjan. Eyewitnesses said bodies were lying on the streets. The shooting started before dawn, with sustained exchanges of heavy machine-gun fire and mortar barrages in several areas of the city. Military sources told Reuters that more than twenty soldiers and civilians had died, adding that the toll was likely much higher. The BBC's Paul Welsh reported from Abidjan that the government appeared to have regained control of key areas of the city, but that the town of Bouake, north of Abidjan, was still under rebel control. Three national football teams were trapped in a Bouake hotel. Footballers from Senegal, Gambia, and Sierra Leone were in the country for a tournament that had now been suspended. This was scary!

I could hardly eat nor sleep. Mercy had come back to Liberia during this same time, but I had to travel by myself. In the midst of this entire turmoil, she made some calls to the Ivory Coast, and I was taken to a hotel. Mercy and her husband comforted me as best as they could from afar. I was on the Ivory Coast for five days, knowing that God was not going to fail me. With the help of the Lord, we managed to leave the country in the midst of all that war trouble. When I got to New York, I lost my ticket, and I had to lodge with a family I travelled with from the Ivory Coast for one night. My son-in-law, Bishop Horace, took care of me. I didn't have to purchase a new ticket. God positioned Bedell and Mercy in two locations to get me out of this situation. Praise God for them. Can you image how I felt: my first time traveling to America, and I find myself in another war situation? God will never reveal his plan ahead of its time. I did not make it for Christmas but arrived the day after. All to his glory! "America, here I come," I said. The first family I met was Reverend Gordon Ogden in Baton Rouge, Louisiana, and his wife, Pat. They were very kind to me.

When it is time for a certain transition in life, nothing can stand in the way. I could not return to Liberia after my visit due to the severity and the intensity of the civil war in Liberia. My life in the USA was very useful to the glory of God. I began my first job at the food service department at Baton Rouge General and also at A&M Southern University in Baton Rouge. My passion for food service management grew tremendously, which made me begin a course at the Culinary Institute in California. At that time, I was residing with one of my daughters, Dayanah Thomas. I completed my studies in Houston, Texas. Little did I know I would use it in helping to run the Alpha Child Development Center and the food pantry and adult day care at Living Word Ministries International. I also followed my dream in education and attended a child development associate program in Houston, Texas. That also qualified me with DFPS to be a licensed director at Alpha Child Development Center.

I am certainly sure that I will use all that I have learned in America in Liberia, and Liberia will be proud of me one day. I am glad that I can let everyone else in the world know just how much I have learned and that my experiences in life will and can be shared with many.

Reflection of America.............My Life in America

Mom first Sunday in America welcome by Sunday school department

Mom visit to the USA bible study in the home of Pastor Gordon

MARTHA ZEAH GARKPI

Family life in USA

Global Evangelism Fellowship

At her grand twins whom she helped raise in Ghana for a year
Emmanuel and Emmuel's graduation (promise keeper)

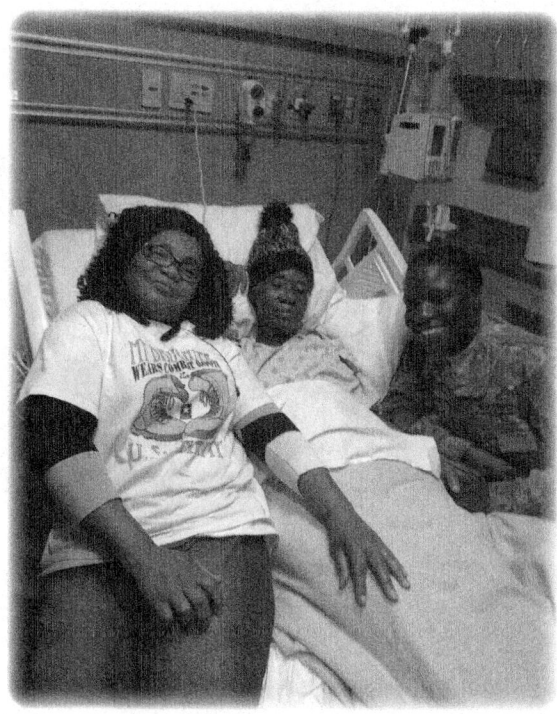

Mom kept her promise for granddaughter to return from Iraq

MARTHA ZEAH GARKPI

Mom attended granddaughter's wedding ceremony (promise keeper)

Mom and granddaughter at boot camp ceremony

Black History Month Celebration 2015 - Mother and daughter

Mother of the Year a Living Word Ministry, Baton Rouge

MARTHA ZEAH GARKPI

(Director at Alpha child Development Center)
from August 2010- May 2017

When I landed in the United States of America in December of 1990, the beauty of this awesome land and the uniqueness of the citizens were apparent. The American society was just as I imaged it to be when I was in Monrovia, Liberia. I arrived in Baton Rouge, LA where I lived with my daughter Kosiapoe and her family, along with a host of friends and church families. We moved to Houston, TX after a while.

Life is amazing in this country. Everywhere I went, there was an abundance of beautiful souls I had the pleasure of interacting with. I have a host of family members, friends and brothers and sisters in Christ all across the nation - Minnesota, California, Massachusetts, Pennsylvania, Delaware, Illinois, Rhode Island, New York, New Jersey, and South Carolina. I took great joy in visiting everyone during my travels. There are so many people I've visited over the years, that I cannot name them all! You all have made my travels well worth it, and the memories will be with me for many years to come.

When I lived with my daughter Judy in Minnesota, I had seen snow for the first time. During the summers, we would go to the farmer's markets and pick our own produce, just so I could bring African food home to Houston. My late foster father Reverend John K. Demey was also living there at the time with his family, and I would go care for them. My time in California with my daughter Deyanah reminded me of Africa – the temperatures were so warm! We would hit the city and shop until we dropped. Massachusetts weather was reminiscent of Minnesota's snowy climate, and I couldn't wait to get back to my home in Houston. However, my baby girl Degusia kept me entertained. We would talk and watch African movies during the snowstorms to pass the time. There are so many pictures to keep the memories alive.

During my time here in the USA, I asked myself two questions over and over again. What am I aiming to achieve, and where am I going? The answer was always right along my path. I enjoyed every moment with friends, relatives and my children and grandchildren. I accomplished a lot in the places I've worked and lived, and I touched many lives in so many ways. A majority of the Americans I came across had lots of ambition and many dreams. Anything is possible in America, so to speak. This is the home of the self-made man; the American Dream is true. I lived to see my children accomplish theirs, as well as many relatives and friends, and even me.

Over all, I have so much joy in serving the Lord in America. Some people may not understand how joyful it can be to serve the Lord. When I say I have joy, I am not talking about mere happiness or laughter only. I am talking about a way of life. When you give yourself to the things of God, there is a peace beyond understanding. When you have joy in your heart from being a faithful servant of God, it will give you stability in your life that produces hope and blessings. This is why I am enjoying life in the USA. Everywhere God has given me the opportunity to be, I am known as a faithful woman of God. I was not doing it to be seen - that's who I am in the Lord.

Joshua 24:15 "And if it seems evil to you to serve the LORD, choose for yourselves this day whom you will serve, whether the gods which your fathers served that were on the other side of the River, or the gods of the Amorites, in whose land you dwell. But as for me and my house, we will serve the LORD."

Joshua took great delight in serving God, and so do I. David is another good example of a man who took great joy in serving God – especially in worshipping Him. We can see this by his life and by the many praise songs he wrote in the Psalms. I feel like I am just like David in that respect, because I love to praise God.

"Psalm 27:6 And now my head shall be lifted up above my enemies all around me; therefore I will offer sacrifices of joy in His tabernacle; I will sing, yes, I will sing praises to the LORD." This is my life as I worship and served in His kingdom.

I was glad when they said to me, "Let us go into the house of the LORD." I did not let the American Dream to take me away from my service of God. If anything, it drew me closer to it.

I am reminded when David came to offer up sacrifices to God, he did not consider it a burden. Instead, he found joy in every opportunity he had to serve God deeply from within. He understood that everything he had belonged to God, and he was very thankful for the many blessings God had given him. So am I. My children, my families, as well as my friends - I am always grateful to God that He led me in their path.

We should have the same joy today. What can be more important than coming into the house of the Lord and worshiping our God for who he is? What can we be happier about? Our primary motive for coming together as Christians is to worship God. Unfortunately, some Christians go to church for many different reasons. There is nothing wrong with enjoying family and friends at church, but it should not be our priority. Life in America is wonderful with all God is continuing to do through me. I will forever be grateful for being in this country. It will always be the safe haven away from my war-ravaged home.

I am hopeful for the changes that are still to come in my home country Liberia. I hope to return one day to see the transformation for myself. The civil war has left my home ravaged, and the violent memories are etched into my brain forever. I pray that my home can return to its original splendor – to the beautiful home I always have known it to be. Until then, America will be my home away from home.

MARTHA ZEAH GARKPI

CHAPTER SEVEN

Reflections of Elder/Teacher Martha Zeah Garkpi:

August 25, 2017

MARTHA GARKPI WAS one of the most dedicated kindergarten teachers I knew. She had the gift of making learning easier for kids. During the early years in school, the children were excited and eager to learn what was taught to them. Her way of teaching the children to recite their alphabets, the days of the weeks, nursery rhymes, Bible verses, the months of the year, sight words, and so forth was very unique. She followed the curriculum given and brought life to it. She also had a unique way of setting a tone for learning, which of course made learning easier and interesting for the little ones. I was privileged to have had several children and grandchildren in her class. They all enjoyed her teaching as much as she enjoyed their participation in class. She brought joy and excitement during graduation. The gifts from parents and relatives were tokens of appreciation for having their children in Aunt Martha's class. The students whose lives she impacted will always cherish the memories of their beloved Aunt Martha, their Nursery 3 teacher. She was the gateway to Calvary Baptist. Calvary Baptist Church School was blessed to have had this dedicated teacher known as Auntie Martha. She fulfilled her purpose, and her life was not in vain. On a personal account, she proves to be one who was friendly in her encounters with others at work.

She had never looked down on anyone, and she was honest in her dealings with others. She encouraged friends who were disheartened. She was a motivator and was strong-minded to all she was entrusted with. She was committed and dedicated in all duties. She was a very pleasant person to be around. She encouraged you where encouragement was needed, prayed with you when you were in distress, and even volunteered to meet your needs although she was not a wealthy person. What she learned being in kindergarten herself as a student, she passed on to her students. She never allowed her personal feelings to create negative emotions about others. She was very cheerful, even when she was going through something. She had her head lifted up with all hope that there was a light at the end of the tunnel. Apart from her profession as a teacher, she was also a dedicated mother.

She was a breadwinner for her children. She was a disciplinarian, teaching her children what she expected them to be in life. She also taught them to be respectful to all. Most of all, she taught them about knowledge of salvation of life and what it meant to be a true Christian. Moral values were also given to them. She taught them the dignity of true labor. She always persevered in a situation, no matter what was thrown at her. Reflecting back to her early years as a student in Sergeant Kollie Town in Suacoco in Bong County, I remember that Martha was very serious about her studies. She showed me how serious she was in getting an education. She was never satisfied with any low grades. She always did her best, which made a lasting impression on my heart and in the lives of others as her teacher. I'm talking about using a lamp and candlelight to study, burning the midnight oil. Upon my return from the United States of America after graduating from the University of Liberia, I was appointed as principal of Calvary Baptist Church School. There, again, I met Martha as a teacher of Calvary Baptist. I was very excited coming across this studious student. I then knew that I had one of the best teachers.

I remember her making a lasting impression on me when I was a teacher at Sergeant Kollie Town. I knew she would instill in her children the benefits of a good education. She was very good at what she did, both in the classroom, at church, among her peers, and at home.

Even in her personal life, I watched her balance life in many ways. Martha will come to me with some personal issues that have hurt her. I watched her shed tears over the situation, which of course left my eyes watery. After we both shed those tears, the next moment, I see Martha back on balance as though nothing has happened. That's the kind of woman she was.

Martha endeared herself to me in a way that I considered her a daughter. She became so close to my heart that I could share some inner thoughts with her. I watched her raise her children with such love, passion, and tenderness.

Even with the Liberian Civil War, which repatriated some of us to America, Martha kept in close communication with me. When I heard of her illness, my heart was broken. All I could do was encourage her spirit. During the time of her illness, she tried to encourage me and kept my hope alive that everything will work well according to the will of God. She reminded me of a hymn that we both love very much.

It Is Well with My Soul

When peace like a river, attendeth my way,
When sorrows like sea billows roll
Whatever my lot, thou hast taught me to say
It is well, it is well, with my soul
It is well with my soul
It is well, it is well with my soul

To all of the readers of Teacher Martha Garkpi's book, you have chosen an episode of a living testimony. Everything that is imprinted in this book is how she lived, why she lived, and the purpose that God gave her—a life well-lived. No matter the challenges one faces in life, God will bring one out. I pray all readers will be blessed and that her life and legacy will live on. I'm blessed to be a part of this wonderful biography. I have such joy that a student of my days has become a teacher, lived a dedicated life, and now she is a writer.

Principal,

Mrs. Victoria Weah-Tallawford

*   *   *

August 1, 2017

My mother's journey in her illness and her life was a great blessing to me. She kept the faith, and she was not afraid of death. She was a mother, wife, evangelist, elder, motivator, grandparent, sister, teacher, instructor, disciplinarian, and writer. She was an educator, and many trade certificates and titles can be attributed to her life in this world. She loved her children. She loved those who celebrated Christ carefully and passionately. Ms. Martha was a member of many organizations and auxiliaries. She was an elder at Living Word Ministries International. Her devoted services to the house of God was known and felt by many. She cleaned, cooked, and served people, and she worked the food pantry with good documentation and worked the summer food program with the state. She ushered every service and encouraged people to sign in when they came to church with the joke, "So the name will be recorded in the Lamb's Book of Life." She sits faithfully and takes notes during every service and every meeting she attends. She served on the finance committee, and she was everything that the Lord wanted her to be. She was also "Auntie Martha" to the children she taught at Calvary Baptist elementary, junior, and now high school in Monrovia, Liberia. She was "Grandma" to the children of Alpha Child Development Center in Houston, Texas. She was "Elder Martha" and "Grandma" to the church family. She loved each person she encountered in a unique and special way!

MARTHA ZEAH GARKPI

I am very glad that this unique, God-fearing, gentle, and very sweet-hearted woman is and was my mother. She will never be forgotten for the dedicated role she played in my life and upbringing. Those devoted hours she spent with me, telling me that I can be whatever I want to be. She would say, "Kosiapoe, I am very proud of you." I say she was proud of herself because she taught me to be hardworking and zealous at whatever I put my hands on, and that was her. Failure was not a part of my DNA. I am glad that she will forever be my mother. I always wanted to teach the little ones because my mother did it very successfully. I am glad that she was right there in Baton Rouge, Louisiana, on May 11, 2001, to see me obtain a Bachelors of Science degree in Early Learning Education (Child Development). Every parent needs someone to carry on their legacy. I called her "Sister" because being the first child in the home, I said what I heard the older people say. Later, I knew it was unique because she was truly that big sister I did not have, and I was that close little sister she did not have. My mother is and was my best friend. I will miss our many adventures together. I did enjoy her company, and she did mine as well. I miss her every day, and I know she misses me too. But with her being in the place that she is now, I'm not worried. I am very proud to have been her eldest daughter and was very privileged for the many opportunities she enabled me to help care for her girls. They are all successful today, and I am very thankful to God. Even in your earthly absence, I will prayerfully keep my promise to you as you have asked of me, "Please take care of your sisters. You're their mother now." I pray that God will enable me to show love and concern for all my sisters. I am so thankful for my dear mother Martha for making a perfect choice in choosing a helpmate and a life partner for me. Her godly advice led me to keep the faith and remain in full-time ministry today, like my mother rightly said, "preaching right alongside her husband, Bishop Bedell Horace." This awesome union you made gave us four wonderful children named Layziadiah Niomie Horace (the first and middle name after your grand-auntie Mamie), Marian Gbaiwon Horace Hill (Gbaiwon, named after your biological mother), Emmuel Mercy Zeah-Wanga Horace (Zeah, named after you), and Emmanuel Bedell Zoeleeckly Horace (Zoeleeckly, named after your only brother by your mother and father). Thank you for your dedicated service to my family and me. If I could have had the earthly power to have kept my mother here, I would. Every medical and spiritual intervention was done. However, you were ready to meet your Maker, and nothing could have held you back. I am grateful to God for taking on such a tasking project in the time of bereavement to convey an overdue, heartfelt message to the world.

My mother lived her life knowing that this world was not her home. Like a songwriter wrote in Liberia, "Let me live my life for Jesus before is too late." There was nothing left undone. Her services were well-done and pleasing to God! In the house, Lord, her children, people she came in contact with, family members, friends—name it, and she left a mark!

Readers who have their parents alive, please honor and give your parents their flowers before it is late, especially if they are dear, caring, and devoted parents. It does not matter the distance, the gap that has been created—it can be mended in true love. Why? They are your parents. After it is all said and done, you will be left with beautiful memories of how you love them.

Pastor Mercy Kosiapoe Horace, daughter

*　　*　　*

August 27, 2017

It is a privilege, honor, and blessing to share the life of this great woman of God.

Our friendship started during our early elementary days in Mid-Baptist Mission in Tappita. Although my sister was several months older, we were very best friends that would confide in each other our top secrets as young girls growing up.

My sister Martha and I grew much closer together when we were always on the same team playing "nayfoot" (one of the most popular games those days that involved several players) during recess. She was one of the best players! She knew the game well.

When we both found out that we were related, originally from Graie, specifically from the same quarter, that brought us even closer together. Henceforth, we named each other *Graie Lay*, meaning "Graie Woman."

In Pa Demey's house, there were four of us that were very close. We did everything together. When you see one person, you see the other three—namely, Martha Garkpi, Martha Demey, Nancy Demey, and Martha Mendoabor. We were the "Great Four." In 1968, we were painfully separated. Our school in Tappita runs from primary through elementary. Our parents didn't want us to attend a non-Christian school.

Since Nancy and Martha Demey and I were one grade ahead of Martha, Nancy and Martha Demey and I were sent off to school in Monrovia. My sister later went to Suakoko Mission along with my sister Darlene, Hannah Demey, and Sarah Kpah to continue her schooling.

However, we were reunited when she was sent to the Thompsons, a missionary family that served at ELWA. We were so happy to be together again. When we would visit each other, when one takes a friend halfway, the other will, in turn, take her halfway. We would be going back and forth all night, not knowing when to stop.

Then we both fell in love with two best friends that were attending Booker Washington Institute (BWI). Martha fell in love with Rufus, and I was in love with Melvin Ngwayah.

Whenever the BWI Glee Club would come to participate in Youth for Christ in Monrovia, we all would be there. Youth for Christ was a Bible quiz program for high schools in Liberia. Well, after graduating from high school, Martha and Rufus got married, and of course, the two best friends were their best man and maid of honor. Our friendship grew stronger and stronger as we became adults. Melvin and I got married a few years later. We would go to movies with Martha and Rufus and do a lot of things together.

At one point, we went to a movie called *Jesus Christ Superstar*. Bad idea! We were very disappointed because it was not we expected to be. In fact, we left when it started. My sister was not just a friend or a sister, but a dear mother to me. I remembered when I had my first child, she moved to my house for two weeks and taught me how to bathe, take care of, and nurse a baby. As a matter of fact, I was very afraid at first that I might break the baby's arm or leg. She held the baby by the leg and said, "Look, his bones are strong like ours. It won't break." Of course thereafter, she was always there to assist me whenever I had baby. She was my children's first nursery teacher, mother, and mentor.

Martha has a sense of humor. She will always make you laugh with her jokes. I could narrate so many of her jokes but one that stuck to me is: There was this well-dressed lady in church, singing along with others from the hymn book, "Count Your Blessings and See What the Lord Has Done." She had the hymn book upside-down, singing to the top of her lungs. There was this little girl standing by her and told her, "Ma, you got the book upside down." She turned to the girl saying, "Child, if you don't sing upside down, you don't sing at all!"

Martha was a loving sister and mother, peacemaker, encourager, courageous woman, and educator. I'm forever grateful and thankful to God know of this loving hero!

Mrs. Martha Ngwayah

*   *   *

August 27, 2017

When we were very young, my sister and I lived with our grandparents Mr. and Mrs. Garkpi. She was just a few years older than me but cared for me tenderly. I remembered when we were living with my parents, Reverend and Mrs. John Demey at the Mid Baptist Mission in Tappita. We always looked forward to the weekend, when we would visit our grandparents on the farm. It was a few miles from Tappita. There were several older boys and girls living with my parents, but she and I were very close. Even when she moved down to Monrovia, we were still in contact until I joined her several years later. One particular thing I know about her was that she was never weary of doing good, not only for her close relatives, but to strangers as well. She copied that from our late father Reverend John Demey. I am proud that she was my sister.

When I was involved in a motor accident while in my teenage years, she was one of five people who donated blood to me, which enabled me to be alive today. I am indeed grateful to all of them. She was always putting others first. I will really miss her.

Mr. Peter Demey

*　　*　　*

September 3, 2017

My dear and loving sister, may your soul rest in perfect peace. I love you dearly, but God loves you best. We were sisters who loved each other so dearly that we could not do anything without consulting each other. Even when our children did anything that did not please or hurt us, we always share and tell each other our feelings. We would then console each other and overcome whatever had happened. That's how we were. I love and miss my sister so much because we were like twin sisters. We never frowned at each other one day in our lives. Now you are gone, and I am left alone. I have no one to share my thoughts with. My dear sister, I love you, and we will meet again in that beautiful land where there is no sickness, pain, or death. May you again rest in perfect peace. Dear, I am missing your sweet tone of voice and jokes.

Love you,

Madame Rebecca B. Mayou

*   *   *

July 22, 2017

Martha Garkpi: A Godly and Virtuous Woman

Who can find a virtuous woman like Martha Zeah Garkpi? For her price is far above rubies.

The heart of her family doth safely trust in her so that they shall not need spoil.

She did her family good and did no evil in all the days of her life.

She seeks wool and flax and works willingly with her hands.

She was like the merchants' ships—her home did not lack anything; it all came from above.

She was ever ready to meet the need of her family, whether day or night.

She lived not in fear. She invested in her tomorrow by laying a good foundation for the children and other lives she touched.

She stood firm, and every ligament of her body shows her strength.

She was very positive at heart and never allowed her challenges to detour her life journey.

She was very determined and was never willing to let go.

She stretched out her hands to the poor and was always giving to the needy in every aspect of her life.

She was not afraid to labor for her household in any given season to see them blessed.

She was always presentable in her outward appearance; her clothing was special.

Her children were known in each community and among the elders of the land.

She was a hard-working woman. She used her hand to deliver blessings into her home.

Strength and honor were her clothing, and she is now rejoicing in the presence of her King.

When she opened her mouth, she spoke with wisdom, and in her tongue was the law of kindness.

She looketh well to the ways of her family, and all who have seen her did not eat the bread of idleness.

Her children rose up and called her blessed, and all whose lives she also touched praise her.

Many daughters have done virtuously, but the mother, elder, teacher, the evangelist—the counselor Ma Martha excelled them all.

Favour is deceitful, and beauty is vain, but a woman that feareth the Lord, like Elder Martha Garkpi, she shall be praised, and her life shall live on forever.

Give her of the fruit of her hands; that she had. And let her works praise her in the gates just as it was when she was departing this world.

Heaven rejoices greatly and pours down showers of blessings upon all who came to witness her glorious departure to glory. She was received in heaven with a shout of powerful lightning and thunder as she said farewell to all who came to celebrate her homegoing. I will miss you for all your love shown to me as a trusted son-in-law, your service in the house of the Lord at Living Word Ministries International, our friendship, and how you entrusted your family in my care. Thanks, and see you soon, "Big Ma" (as I called you)!

Bishop Bedell L. Horace, your pastor

CONCLUSION

MY BOOK, *MARTHA'S Story*, is a testimony of my faith as a child of God. I am inspired to narrate the story of my life because more than anything, it shows the hand of God at work in one person among men in a way that manifests the power, love, divine purpose, and character of our creator. The events of difficulty, abandonment, and disappointment that I encountered could have been meaningless without the clear and unequivocal direct and indirect interventions by the Almighty. The interplay of my difficulties and the hand of God in my life enabled me to live a full and fruitful life. In all, God blessed me with four beautiful daughters, carried me through the death and destruction of the Liberian Civil War, life as a refugee, and migration to the United States. My hope and desire is that my life's story, *Martha's Story*, will serve as an inspiration to other women and girls, and help enable them to understand and be certain in the knowledge that with God, all things are possible. Stand strong in all that you do, because you are a child of the Most High God! He will make you the head and not the tail. You will be above and not beneath. Don't let your circumstances overcome you. Fight the good fight of faith. Don't let the enemy see you down. You can fall, but don't stay down. Don't make decisions in haste. Always go to the Lord in prayer for clarity, and be willing to accept his answer.

AUTHOR'S NOTE

OUR OLD FOLKS say when the mountain is small or lower, people pass over it. When the mountain is tall like a hill, people pass over it. When it has become a real mountain, people find a way of getting around it, rather than passing over. It is like life. One has to make the most of their circumstances. When you are young, your eyes pass through things you don't know. What I mean by that is when you make decisions, you don't know the outcome. Acknowledge God as your number 1 in life, and everything else will fall into place. For instance, consider the ins and outs of married life. One will never know whether or not their partner will be faithful to them until death. I don't know if some people understand that having children is not a game to play. Babies are not toys that you play with, and when you get tired of them, you put away into a toy box. No, it does not work like that. When you are young, you think that the world will always be as sweet as it was when you opened your eyes in it. Oh no! My experience is a lesson in life.

The older you grow; your hills grow taller and eventually turn into mountains. That is, the older you become in life, the more you realize that nothing is easy. In some countries, when you are eighteen years old or big enough to be accountable for your own life, you are expected to make life's decisions on your own, be it good or bad. The choice is yours. In my native land, parents do not set a particular time for a grown child to leave the home. If you still act as a child in obedience to your parents, you can stay however long you need. Some of us have it our own way, and as time goes on, it gets us by our neck. Our mountain gets too high, so we go around it rather than over it, by the grace of God. The Bible says, "For there is nothing hidden that will not be disclosed, and nothing concealed that will not be known or brought out into the open." Never pay evil for evil.

As God says, "The secret things belong to the LORD our God, but the things which I have revealed in this lifelong testimony belong to us and to our sons and daughters to learn from for forever; experience is the best teacher. Do not reinvent the wheel when you don't need to. A hint to a wise is quite sufficient." It is not your location in life that matters. It is you that can change your environment to continue to affect people's lives. If you are completely sure of your decisions, remember you have God's blessing—*go for it!*

Never allow any person or anyone to bring you down or prevent you from experiencing what God has for you. Live a life with no regrets and no limits, no matter whatever circumstances life brings your way! God wants you to be extremely happy about life. "That there is none like him on the earth, a blameless and upright man, who fears God and turns away from evil?" God knows who you and I are in this world, and he can and will stand to defend us

Brothers and sisters, whenever you hold fast to Christ, he will give you the will to see you through! If you keep on keeping on, your strength he will renew! Give your all to him because he took us from disgrace to give us grace. He covers our shame with his blood and lets us shine through his light! What has God put you here on earth to do? If you're not sure, ask God, and he will point the way. Thanks to all readers.

CO-AUTHOR'S NOTE

F ROM WHAT I have discovered in my mother's book, it clearly shows her indecisiveness concerning her marriage with hope to hold on expecting a change one day which never came, but rather she held onto an unwavering faith. The indecisive decision led her to an unbalanced life which created an avenue of faith for her to travel upon. Uncharted territories were abundant, and all she could do was walk by faith. Letting God do his due diligence has made room for an amazing story. She has showed me what a true woman of God is, and her legacy will continue to do the same. No matter our past or failures, our destiny was mapped before we were born. Nothing can stop the greatness destined for you! Let my mother's story be a living example of God's great work. He can turn your *mess* into a *message*!

ACKNOWLEDGMENTS

AUNTIE REBECCA MAYU, we can never forget the many sacrifices you've made in the lifetime of our mother from her adulthood until she passed away. Thank you! You are a true sister. Auntie Martha Demey-Mengua, thanks for your daily prayer and contact with your sister. Ms. Shirley Householder, you've shown your love to your friend and sister Martha in so many ways, sitting with her at home and at the hospital whenever she needed you. Auntie Sarah Karbbar, thanks for helping your sister with the home and doctor's visitation when needed and for providing the amazing meals. I remember our wonderful neighbors who fed my mother during the summer of 2017 with awesome meals and special visitations—Dr. and Mrs.Tawfiq Abu-raqabeh, thanks.

Isaac Karto, Grace Biah, Zamgbah Taylor, Mercy Krua, and Joan Davies, you all have shown so much love and generosity to Ma Martha. All of your actions and deeds have been so helpful, and I am forever grateful.

Bishop Bedell Horace, thanks for being that awesome spiritual leader and the wonderful son-in-law she wanted. You set the bar. You were that son in-law she was proud of. You took such wonderful care of your mother in-law, whom you looked to as mother till death. Thank you.

My cousin, Pastor John Beataye Beaye—*the son of my mother's only brother Zobuia*—your auntie was unable to see you in this life; she was very happy to have remained alive to hear from you. The many phone communications were fulfilling to her. There is another place of fellowship that is much better then here.

My beloved sisters—Bley Judy Greaves, Dayanah B. Thomas, and Degusia P. Mulbah—thanks for being very caring and loving to our dear mother in her lifetime. Your love will be forever remembered by her. Never forget the message she delivered to all of us June 2016 at the family reunion in Houston, Texas, and lastly in June 2017 on our mother-and-daughters conference call.

To all my wonderful nieces and nephews, and my children, many thanks for being a part of a dream and fulfillment to your grandmother's legacy. Remember all that she has taught and guided you to be. Please keep your promise to her, Layziadiah, Marian, Emmuel and Emmanuel Horace; Mary and Henry Greaves; Queen-McDyn and Michael Thomas; Bedell, Debleye and Wasima Martha Mulbah; and all of John Beataye-Beaye Yarclay's children.

To my special brothers-in-law—Barkon Greaves, Michael Thomas, and Walter Mulbah—thanks for being the awesome son-in-laws that our mother Martha bragged about. According to her story, she did not have a marital union like the ones she saw in your homes. Shame the devil and make him a liar that divorce and separation will not be the potion of her daughters. Keep your promise to love, support, and cherish your wives as the Bible as instituted it to be, and your lives will be blessed.

SOURCES

AZLyrics. "Audrey Assad Lyrics - It Is Well With My Soul." Accessed October 17, 2017. https://www.azlyrics.com/lyrics/audreyassad/itiswellwithmysoul.html.

BBC News. "Liberia Country Profile." Last modified October 10, 2017. Accessed October 17, 2017. http://www.bbc.com/news/world-africa-13729504.

BBC News UK. "'Coup attempt' in Ivory Coast." Africa. Last modified September 19, 2002. Accessed October 17, 2017. http://news.bbc.co.uk/1/hi/world/africa/2268718.stm.

Bible Gateway. "Proverbs 3:5." Accessed October 17, 2017. https://www.biblegateway.com/passage/?search=Proverbs+3%3A5.

Bible Hub. "Luke 8:17." Accessed October 17, 2017. http://biblehub.com/luke/8-17.htm. "For there is nothing hidden that will not be disclosed, and nothing concealed that will not be known or brought out into the open."

Daily Verses. "Bible Verse of the Day." Accessed October 17, 2017. https://dailyverses.net.

Gray, Cyrus. *Negro Nation: The Love of Liberty Brought Us Here?* Houston: Africa Rising, 2016.

Guannu, Joseph Saye. *A Short History of the First Liberian Republic*, 3rd ed., Monrovia: Star Books, Monrovia, 1985.

Imtiaz, Huma. "US Aid to Sunni Ittehad Council Backfired." *The International Herald Tribune*. In Allgov.com. Accessed October 17, 2017. http://www.allgov.com/departments/independent-agencies/united-states-agency-for-international-development-usaid?agencyid=7290.

Johnston, H. H., and O. Stapf. *Liberia*. London: Hutchinson & Company, 1906.

Josh.org. "Attributes of God." Accessed October 17, 2017. https://www.josh.org/resources/spiritual-growth/attributes-of-god.

Knot, The. "38 Bible Verses About Marriage and Love." Accessed October 17, 2017. https://www.theknot.com/content/bible-verses-about-marriage.

Knowing Jesus Online Bible. "Old Testament." Accessed October 17, 2017. https://bible.knowing-jesus.com.

Lyrics On Demand. "Liberia National Anthem Lyrics." Accessed October 17, 2017. http://www.lyricsondemand.com/miscellaneouslyrics/christianlyrics/thoughyoursinsbeasscarletlyrics.html.

Lyrics On Demand. "Though Your Sins Be As Scarlet Lyrics." Accessed October 17, 2017. http://www.lyricsondemand.com/n/nationalanthemlyrics/liberianationalanthemlyrics.html

McPherson, J. H. T. *History of Liberia*, John Hopkins University Studies in Historical and Political Science, 1891.

Momodu, Samuel. The Black Past: Remembered and Reclaimed. Accessed October 17, 2017. http://www.blackpast.org/contributor/momodu-samuel.

Peace Insight. "Liberia: Conflict and Peace." Accessed October 17, 2017. https://www.insightonconflict.org/conflicts/liberia/conflict-profile.

Pike, John. Global Security. "Liberia - First Civil War - 1989–1996." Accessed October 17, 2017. http://www.globalsecurity.org/military/world/war/liberia-1989.html.

US Agency for International Development (USAID). "Importance of Democracy, Human Rights, & Governance to Development." Democracy, Human Rights and Governance. Accessed October 17, 2017. https://www.usaid.gov/what-we-do/democracy-human-rights-and-governance /importance-democracy-human-rights-governance.

Wikipedia. "1999 Ivorian coup d'état." Accessed October 17, 2017. https://en.wikipedia.org/wiki/1999_Ivorian_coup_d%27%C3%A9tat.

CPSIA information can be obtained
at www.ICGtesting.com
Printed in the USA
BVOW06*1018090218

507732BV00006B/16/P

9 781543 461091